BLAZING SADHUS

or
Never Trust
A Holy Man
Who Can't
Dance

BLAZING SADHUS

or

Never Trust
A Holy Man
Who Can't
Dance

Achyutananda Das

(Charles M. Barnett)

CMB
Books

First printing: October 2012
Second printing: February 2013

Printed in the United States of America

ISBN 978-1-4675-5057-4

To contact the author, please write to:
Charles M. Barnett
P. O. Box 35
Alachua, Florida, USA
32616-0035

Book design and back cover photo by Yamaraj Das

COVER PHOTO: Chanting in Calcutta, 1967.
The author is playing *kartals* (hand cymbals).
Srila Prabhupada is to his right, arms upraised.

DEDICATION

This book is dedicated to my father, who gave me the *Bhagavad Gita* when I was eight years old, and having earned his wings, is probably sitting at God's conference table telling Him just how things ought to be. And to my eternal spiritual father, Srila Prabhupada, who taught me the *Bhagavad Gita*. It is also dedicated to all the souls currently being born in Vaishnava families all over the world.

Acyutananda das

His Divine Grace
A. C. Bhaktivedanta Swami Prabhupada
Founder-*Acarya* of the International Society for Krishna Consciousness

*"He looked like he had the wisdom of the
prime minister of the galaxy."*

CONTENTS

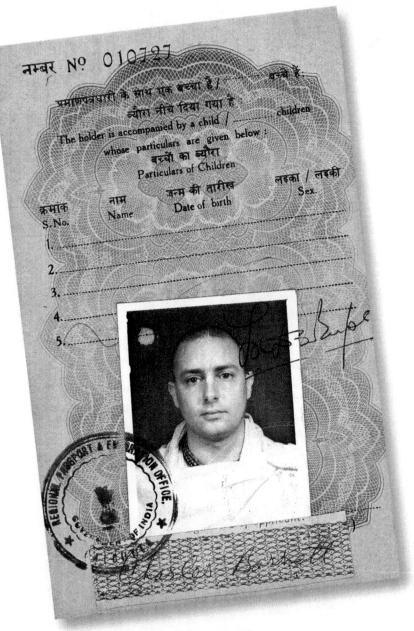

Indian ID Certificate

"You are 99% citizen, you just cannot vote."
—CID officer, Calcutta

PREFACE

Ever since W. Somerset Maugham's *The Razor's Edge,* many books and films have appeared with a similar theme: "Screwed-up Westerner goes to the East, turns native, gets enlightenment"—with most of the emphasis on the screw-up and not much on the enlightenment. My purpose in this autobiographical book is to describe more of the knowledge and wisdom that a disciple receives. Krishna says, "I am situated in everyone's heart and from Me come knowledge, memory, and forgetfulness." Krishna in our hearts sends memories on how to fulfill our desires and withholds memories that hinder them. I hope that Krishna has helped me remember the significant things and forget the useless ones. Some anecdotes and adventures may be fond memories of my own, but others may not find them so. (Ever have to watch a friend of a friend's wedding video?)

There are many quotes in this book that I heard from Srila Prabhupada himself and from others. The best is, "Study my books very carefully, because after I'm gone people will say, 'Prabhupada said this; Prabhupada said that . . .'"

With that in mind, Srila Prabhupada said, "There are sons of the father and sons of the mother. Sons of the mother are attracted to the facilities and assets of the mission. Sons of the father are attracted by the message of their guru." In the eleven years we knew him, his every word or action pushed on the Krishna movement in all its dimensions. Many people became Krishna conscious by having seen Prabhupada only once or having heard a few words that ignited the fire of devotion in their hearts. My progress was slow, and I needed much more—enough to fill a book.

one
Life in New York

I was born in Brooklyn, New York, 1948, of un-Orthodox Jewish parents. My father was a WWII veteran who'd been stationed in the Philippines and Japan, where he developed a sincere appreciation for Asian culture. He showed me his collection of books: *The Upanishads, The Bhagavad Gita,* Haiku poetry, books from the Theosophical Society, and several books on Buddhism and yoga. I read them as much as my eight-year-old mind could understand. My mother was a beautiful blonde, good wife, good mother. Dad told the family he had an Uncle Charlie and insisted on giving me the name Charles. Actually he didn't have an Uncle Charlie; he wanted me named after Charlie Barnet, the famous bandleader, just to give me music. He bought me a toy saxophone and taught me to play "Little Boy Blue." He was an innovative salesman of a variety of products, so we were well off. We had everything. Actually, we had two of everything—two homes, two cars, two TVs . . . too much. When I read *National Geographic's* condescending descriptions of foreign cultures "that haven't changed their way of life for thousands of years," I thought, *Maybe that's because they like it that way.*

11

When I was nine, mother took me to see the Broadway production of *Peter Pan*.

While waiting in line, I asked, "What's Pan mean?"

"The name comes from the Greek god Pan. He never grows old. He lives in the forest and plays the pan flute."

I didn't quite relate to a grown woman (Mary Martin) playing the part of a ten-year-old boy who didn't want to go to school. I did want to grow up. But what if there was a place that you could fly to just by thinking happy thoughts? What if there was a place where you'd never age and have fun perpetually? What if . . . ? Nah! Of course, my mother wanted me to be educated, but I was beginning to see that school and education might be two different things. On the cover of a schoolbook I wrote, "Don't let school interfere with your education."

One night I heard my parents bickering bitterly in the living room. I kept silent in my room. When the arguing stopped, there was only silence in the house. After a while, my father called me into the bathroom. He was sitting in the tub, warm water up to his waist.

"Charles," he asked, "is the lotus position right foot over the left or the left foot over the right?"

"I think you're supposed to alternate 'em." I said.

He needed peace of mind, something more to life than just owning material things and being entertained, more than just being well off.

When my father was selling dealerships for Japanese tape recorders, his sales strategy was to walk the streets of Manhattan soliciting ground-floor storeowners. However, most of the stores had signs that said NO SOLICITORS, so he began looking to the businesses on the second and third floors. One was the laboratory of Dr.

Marius Bohun Greene. The doctor bought two tape recorders. My dad had some health conditions that the doctor helped him with, and they became friends. Dr. Greene, then in his seventies, was the leading anesthesiologist in, probably, the world. His books are still studied in the medical field. Dr. Greene's mother was Hungarian and his father Irish. He often sat on the dais with the grand master of the Ancient Order of Hibernians at the St. Patrick's Day parade in New York. The title Bohun can be traced to British tribal antiquity. The doctor calculated that if a certain three hundred or so people died, he would be next in line to the throne of England. Dr. Greene had his eccentricities. He drove an ambulance instead of a car. "So I can park anywhere," he said in his Hungarian accent. He wore a Vandyke beard, one ruby earring, and under his vest, a .357 magnum revolver. "It can stop a Volkswagen." His home and second laboratory was a beautiful mansion in Queens, New York.

One evening the doctor invited my father and me to dinner. I wandered through his gorgeously furnished rooms. Every piece of furniture and knickknack was an heirloom of the old Europe. One room was screened off and converted into an aviary of exotic birds. He bought the tape recorders to record the songbirds.

After dinner the doctor showed me a cabinet that held a collection of pipes. One long pipe was intricately carved in the shape of a dragon.

Pointing to the pipe, I asked him, "What is this for?"

"Oh, that. That is for opium. Opium nothing much, it give you euphoria."

Dr. Greene sat down in his favorite leather chair and began to read softly from a huge leather-bound volume of *Don Quixote* in the original Spanish, and invited me to sit with him. He saw me staring at a framed photograph on the wall. It was a picture of him, much younger, standing amidst a line of bearded Russian soldiers. They wore long great coats and had huge black pistols tucked into their belts.

"I was the medic to Stalin's bodyguards. This boy in the middle was seven feet tall and still growing!"

And then he said in a euphoria of his own, "You know, Charlie, I have seen over five thousand deaths, but maybe only ten or twelve people died with dignity."

Like the chairs, this moment was priceless. I could only nod with some bit of understanding of what he meant; fear of death or indignity.

On the way home all I thought about was exotic Haiku Zen poems, Hindu books called *Gita* and *The Upanishads,* Vedanta peace of mind, and especially EUPHORIA! My favorite definition of euphoria: "When your mind starts reeling and a-walking, your inside voice starts squealing and a-squawking, floating around on a belladonna cloud singin' Euphoria."

One Haiku book had a Japanese brush painting of a high cliff and a waterfall. Standing at the base was an old sage with a crooked staff, at peace with the world. That's what I want to be when I grow up.

When I was fourteen years old my grandfather died. We called him Papa Lou. He made his first fortune as a boxing promoter in the '20s until, while he was handling a promising fighter, a gangster slapped him on the back: "You just got a partner." Then Papa Lou got out of the fight game.

My grandmother, Carrie, was a Roman Catholic from Bavaria. The family moved from Austria and Germany to England in the

1880s when all British, even royals, had to change their Teutonic names to British titles. Jewish families liked the change; it helped them assimilate into European British culture. That's how I get the name Barnett, and that's why grandpa was laid out in a Catholic funeral parlor. At the funeral I was suited up, hair cut, shiny shoes. We stood around with relatives and friends, business partners, and an old time boxer. Washing up in the men's room, I noticed that some of my uncles had tattooed numbers on their forearms. The newsreels were true.

My father took me aside, and we sat together in a pew.

"People expect the father and son to go up to the coffin together. Don't feel at all disturbed," my father told me as he gestured towards the suited body in the coffin. "This is not Papa Lou, the person. This is—although it doesn't sound so nice—just the remains. We are not a person with a soul; we are a soul covered by a body." Dad had been reading the *Bhagavad Gita*. He also said, "Jesus said that too, to Nicodemus: 'the soul is like the wind that bloweth, and we hear the sound of it but can't tell from where it comes from,' or something like that. The *Gita* says the same thing in another way. It goes sort of like "All beings are visible in their beginning, visible in their living state, and become invisible again after they die. So what need is there for lamentation?"

We stood as father and son before the open casket and saw my grandfather's remains. I was not disturbed.

I appreciated that at the end of the *Gita*, Krishna tells his student-friend Arjuna, "Now deliberate on what I have said, and do as you feel fit." This appealed to me more than the last words of the Old Testament: "Lest I smite the earth with a curse."

I attended James Monroe High School, which had an excellent

music department. I took up the flute. I was listening to flutists Yusef Latif and Herbie Mann. Mr. Emil Greenburg, head of the music department, was a teacher, conductor, and mentor to anyone serious about a career in music. He wanted me to play the saxophone, but to me the sax had the timbre of a chromatic car horn in three-plus octaves. I couldn't picture a sage playing a sax, so I chose the primeval flute. Mr. Greenburg introduced us to various forms of music, their modes, themes, and history.

In one class he said, "The most beautiful melody in the world is the C major scale. Each note has a shape, an emotion, a color, and a purpose, even a taste. Everybody repeat, *do re mi fa so la ti . . . ti . . . ti.* Ya hear that? That pull, that anxiety, that longing? You gotta come to that safe, restful, no-place-like *do!*"

He often said, "What makes a song great is when you hear the melody and the words immediately come to mind. And when you hear the words the melody comes to mind."

At one rehearsal of Beethoven's First Symphony, he slammed his baton down on his music stand and yelled, "Everybody stop!"

He took a long sigh and said, "Look, you don't play music *on* an instrument. You make music come *out* of the instrument. *Kapeesh?*"

We kapeeshed.

"So, this time I don't want to hear any instruments, I don't want to hear any notes, I don't want to hear any chords, I don't even want to hear the melody; I just want to hear the emotions. Now, start again."

We sounded great. That's called learning.

Several students were already professionals. Nydia Charo became a superstar in Puerto Rico. Artie at sixteen was already playing bass in jazz bands.

One day Mr. Greenburg called me into his office. He took off his jacket, rolled up his sleeves, and lit up a cigar.

"Look kid," he said, "you're a flute player and a good one, but this can be a dirty business. I was playing a gig in some hotel and had found some great music arrangements, and I sat in the green room for days copying them. Next to the table was a cot so filthy I didn't want to touch it, let alone do the things some people had been doin' on it. So, some day you're gonna be out there starving, you're gonna go play in some Cuban rumba band, but the drummer's gotta a cousin who also plays the flute, so he's gonna say you're a white kid with no sense of rhythm, and he's going to make life miserable for you. Did you play last week? How much did you make?"

"Twelve-fifty and a sandwich."

"Kid, I don't go on the floor for less than fifty bucks. You gotta gear up and study."

I nodded. The picture of the music world didn't look all that bright, but what career was? That's why they call it work. I could see the struggle was in any career, but this one had music. So I studied hard, played a lot, and got better than just good.

Mr. Greenberg got us student-priced tickets to all of the great performances in New York. I attended one of the only three live performances of John Coltrane playing "My Favorite Things." Mr. Coltrane was standing stone-still on the stage at the Ninety-Second Street Young Men's Hebrew Association (YMHA). The only thing moving were his fingers. Drummer Elvin Jones was sweating through his suit. I sat in the front row looking straight up the bell of Trane's soprano saxophone. This performance was a revolution in music of any style. It changed people's lives. He leaped from the standard hap-hap-happy Broadway show tune into whirling dervishes of sounds never heard this side of the Nile. This performance inspired people to read Buddhism, Taoism, and Sufi mysticism. I don't know if Julie Andrews would have understood or approved of it.

Two verses in the *Bhagavad Gita* in particular kept pulling at me like the seventh note of the C major scale. "By Me this entire universe is pervaded. All beings are in Me, but I am not in them." The next verse compounded the paradox: "And yet, everything that is created does *not* rest in Me. Behold My mystic opulence." What does that mean? This was too much for my puppy brain. In the Theosophical Society edition of the *Gita* was a line-drawing of young Krishna surrounded by animals, demons, and angelic forms. He was wearing a long pearl necklace. The caption read, "Know that I pervade these universes like pearls on a thread." I can see the necklace, I thought, but I can't see the thread. There must be a logical explanation. Who am I to apply logic?

In chapter fifteen, verse fifteen, Krishna describes Himself as the author, the knower, and goal of all the *Vedas* and *Vedanta*. That word *Vedanta* appeared in other books of yoga and the *Upanishads* and was esoterically described as "the conclusion of all knowledge." I thought that would be nice to have, certainly more useful than high school algebra.

Elsewhere the *Gita* said, "Try to learn the Truth by approaching a spiritual master. Inquire from him submissively and render service to him. The self-realized soul can impart the knowledge unto you because he has seen the truth." Even a book on sword fencing said, 'One must learn from a master, not a book.' But how would I know what a "self-realized soul" would act or look like? A Franciscan monk? A Buddha in jeans? Or like no one special, hiding his wisdom for only other enlightened ones?

I envisioned Dominic, our Italian handyman, fixing the sink and telling me of the wisdom of the ages he'd learned in his former lives as a Chinese general, an Apache shaman, or a Tibetan Lama. I met Dominic in the elevator.

"Do you ever ask 'what does it all mean, why are we here?'"

Dominic replied, "I just do what I gotta do; that's all I know."

The *Gita* described a realized soul as being indifferent to pleasure and pain. "Birth, death, and rebirth are considered temporary minor disturbances." Death a minor disturbance! All the enlightened souls were happy in any condition. Or maybe on some day while I saw a rose or watched *I Love Lucy,* everything would fall into place and I'd fill with cosmic consciousness and walk around with a nauseating smile fixed on my face. I started observing everyone—teacher, hipster, bum on the street—in the light of what I read.

"Whatever it is, I'm against it."—Groucho Marx

My father took me to Greenwich Village, the cosmopolitan area of New York City, far more eclectic than the provincial Bronx. The girls were prettier too, no hairspray. Even today the streets and houses look like Paris. We read poetry and *Dissent* magazine and searched *Cue* magazine for interesting events. They all led us to cafe's and dives in The Village. I started going to these joints alone and became familiar with the hot and cool places and some of the characters who frequented or performed in them. Brother Theodore, an angry Slavic monologist: "The only thing that keeps me going is the hope of dying young!" Hugh Romney, who later mellowed and morphed into the clown Wavy Gravy: "We are climbing Harpo's ladder." The overall message was that this reality is not good enough. Nonconformity was liberating; pessimism was raised to an art form.

Yes, everybody remembers where they were when they heard the news of JFK's assassination on November 22, 1963. I was in high school when the announcement came over the school PA speaker that Kennedy had been shot, and then a few minutes later we heard Walter Cronkite's choked voice tell us he died. I thought, *This changes everything. This is the dawning of the Age of Chaos. Ain't it great!*

I wanted to hear what the hip poets and thinkers made of the event. During the hour-long subway ride to the Village, fear and solemnity set in.

In the '50s, Americans felt confident and safe. We weren't, but we felt that way. One morning my second-grade teacher came into the classroom and cheerfully greeted us. "Good morning boys and girls." Then she extended her arms, slapped her hands together and shouted, "Take cover!" That meant to scramble under our desks and giggle. After a short while, the teacher said reassuringly, "All clear." In the '50s men wore wide-brimmed fedora hats. It was rumored they would protect you from radioactive fallout—Strontium-90. In 1960 JFK was elected. He never wore hats—"All clear!"

After the announcement of the Dallas assassination, the school let us all go home. In Washington Square all the enlightened intellectuals were benumbed, crying, and sobbing like it was the end of the world. There was no music on Macdougal Street that night. One "pristine bullet" and they were devastated. I was very disappointed in my friends who claimed to know all the answers.

Someone cried out, "This is the end of Camelot!"

Splivy the drummer, who got his name from Miles Davis, yelled at the group of mourners who sat on park benches, "What's with this Camelot? What, we got some kinda king and queen down there in DC? Don't we got a democratic government? You know, by the people, of the people, and *on* the black people?"

"Y'know," he said, "y'all don't look so hip no more."

Dad had a collection of exotic knives and fine tobacco pipes. My mother's Freudian symbology kicked in, and she would complain, "Penises! Phalluses! Sigmund Freud says it means sex and death."

Dad's vocabulary included words like *satori, nirvana, tao, shanti realization, peace of mind.* He quoted the *Gita,* D.T. Suzuki, and Alan Watts. My mother used words like catharsis, complex, transformative, well-balanced, subconscious, and therapeutic. She quoted Adler and Freud. My dad quit coming home. My parents agreed to part. They divorced. Dad remarried, went to California, and became very successful. I stayed with my mother in New York. She worked and studied psychology at New York University, her courses maddening me by interpreting everything as a symbolic representation of something other than itself. My mother went on to earn her degree and become head of admissions of Daughters of Jacob Nursing Home. I went on doing yoga.

I perfected the *hatha*-yoga exercises, including the difficult *nauli* sequence. For weeks I did breathing exercises, rolling the stomach and torso, inhaling and exhaling, pressing out the navel, drawing in the navel. Then one day in the standing position, both hands placed on my knees, saturated with oxygen so I could last the thirty seconds minimum without any dizziness, the sub-abdominal rectal muscles were drawn to the surface. This creates a suction that awakens the flow of *kundalini.* (And if you sit in a tub of water, you can give yourself an enema, but remember to get out of the tub in time.)

When I saw those muscles, at first it was a little scary, but it was inspiring to know that the yoga process is real.

I studied yoga, meditated on the sacred sound *om,* designed my own *mandalas* (symmetrical geometric diagrams), and stared at them until the shapes burned into my brain. There were very few yoga schools at that time, so I could only go by my instincts. The yoga books said the *ajna chakra,* situated in the forehead, would lead one to a guide. I practiced concentrating on that one. In all mystic disciplines the human body is described as the microcosm of the universal planetary systems. "As above, so below." Each universe has lower, middle, and upper whorls of planetary systems, and the body has six *chakras,* or wheels of influences that affect the various human endeavors: (1) digestion and evacuation, (2) reproduction, (3) balance, creation, and destruction (known as the Dan Tien in Tai Chi, Shingyi, Chi Gung, and other Chinese disciplines), then (4) emotional, (5) communicative, (6) intuitional and enlightenment. They are described as lotuses, each having a number of petals according to the number of qualities and properties each whorl possesses. (For example, in the Ayurveda medical system the human heart is described as a drooping lotus bud. The heart does look like that.) These blossoms of energy cannot be found by medical examinations or by autopsy and are rejected by western science, since no gross evidence is observable by these blunt methods. An autopsy will only reveal arteries and organs, no lotuses.

But I came to an analogy of my own while staring at a subway map of Manhattan. You see the path of the tunnels and streets as numbered lines and stations printed horizontally, diagonally, and vertically. You can't tell from the map that Broadway and Forty-Seventh Street is the theatre district. You can't tell by looking at the map that Wall Street and Broad Street are the center of the financial district. However, people who work in these fields see it with their professional vision. To be "on Wall Street" doesn't mean taking the subway to the station. You will only see buildings. One has to be qualified, obtain a series of seven brokers licenses, and be hired by a broker/dealer and trade. Likewise to be "on Broadway" you have to be a talented professional actor, dancer, singer. Then you practice, practice, practice. Get an agent, follow a director, learn lines, and so on.

Raising the life force, the *kundalini,* by the yoga process is highly codified and must be directed by a teacher, and one must ritually please the presiding gods and goddesses who reside in them. Without this guidance the reactions can be far worse than a white-collar criminal's penalty for insider trading. But more about that later. Much more.

I guess my *chakras* were blooming because the high school compared my below-average grades to my 142 IQ and declared me an under-achiever. I think I was achieving things that the Board of Education didn't find helpful in becoming a productive citizen. I graduated in June 1965, and stayed with my mother in her apartment in Greenwich Village. I ignored the pressure of my mother to go to college.

"Mom, I've been sitting at a desk for twelve years. I'm going to get a job and play music."

I did get a job filling orders from bookstore owners to a book distribution warehouse called Bookazine. I enjoyed helping the bookstore owners who called in for copies of the "Ba-hah-ga-, Ba-ha . . ."

"*Bhagavad Gita,*" I said.

"Yeah. Ten copies. Penguin paperback."

I found my musical voice playing with Richie Havens up and down the cafés on Macdougal Street. The famous Café Wha? had a Saturday afternoon hootenanny, which meant you didn't get paid. I was calling myself Chuck. There were folk singers, and folk singers, and a few more folk singers. Bob Dylan came in once, drunk, and the owner threw him out. The next day Bob Dylan's album came out and it was a super hit. The owner of the Café Wha? wept bitter tears. I went every weekend. One day I played with an army of Conga drummers. Richie Havens sat in the back in the dark, looking over huge art sketchbooks. Richie would often be seen on Sixth Avenue charging two dollars for charcoal portraits of tourists. After my set he called me over, "Hey Chuck!" and showed me his portfolio. There were 24" x 18" pages of his charcoal and pencil sketches. The first one was a very realistic drawing of the crucifixion of Jesus Christ. The second was the crucifixion of Jesus, slanted obliquely. The third was the crucifixion only in dark shades. One page had the scene of the three crucifixions where all three were Jesus, without the thieves. Page after page of crucifixions. Ritchie wore a cluster of over a dozen tiny gold and silver crucifixes around his neck. His guitar was held in shape by yards of shiny black electrician's tape.

"Hey Chuck," he'd say, "could you give me a nickel? I need to get on the Path subway to get to Jersey."

"Sure."

He would spend all his money on new guitar strings that would snap from his heavy-handed strumming style. He invited me to play with him. I liked his playing because he wasn't imitating anybody. There were terrific musicians who referred to their music styles as "influenced by" or "borrowed from." Actually they were stealing, but always introduced their songs as original compositions. All wanted to hit the big time, but to sell out was anathema. The whole scene was confusing.

I saw Buffy Saint-Marie, the famous Native American folk singer, walk across Washington Square Park in a full business suit and high heels. I remained sitting in the café listening to singers, poets, and comedians. Bill Cosby, Lenny Bruce, and Richard Pryor all passed through on their way up. Others stagnated or faded into oblivion.

"Both the lowest fools and those in the transcendental perfection of intelligence enjoy happiness. Those in between suffer."

—*Srimad Bhagavatam*, 3000 BCE

(I was definitely in between.)

Monarchies Have Court Jesters, Democracies Have Stand-Up Comics

One day Richard Pryor's manager asked me to play a gig to open a new movie theater in New Jersey. Ritchie Havens, Pryor, a folk singer, the manager, and I packed into a car. Pryor was always jumpy. He made everybody nervous. After our set, he did an X-rated monologue to a Saturday morning audience of ten-year-olds. We sat in the front row, passed a joint, and watched a full hour of Daffy Duck cartoons. Euphoria! On the car trip back, the radio reported on the Russian Sputnik satellite. Pryor turned back to me from the front seat.

"Hey, Chuck!" (meaning the white boy from the Bronx with the flute) "I think when they get to the moon, all the people on the moon are gonna look like one big ugly hairy piece of shit floatin' around. What you think?"

"I . . . I don't know."

"You don't *know*? You don't *know!?*" he shouted. "Baby, I pay you to know!"

I looked out the window of the car at the bleak New Jersey landscape and said to myself, *This is not "The Way."*

"For there is nothing either good or bad, but thinking makes it so."

—Hamlet

The Fat Black Pussy Cat—The Cat for short—was the largest coffee house in the Village. Its entrance was on Macdougal Street, and the café extended through the block to the back door on Minetta Lane. This provided a convenient escape for anyone evading narco detectives, angry lovers, or just any annoying person you didn't like. Dark even at midday, the only light was from candles in straw-wrapped Chianti bottles. Some of the tables were chessboards and you were free to assemble the chairs and tables any way you liked.

In this salon of intellectualism, men and women who could finish *The New York Times* crossword puzzle in ten minutes propounded some of the most preposterous ideas. What was so extraordinary was how they spoke with such conviction and authority, or sometimes just louder than everyone else.

"Eschatology, ontology, epistemology, violence, nonviolence— it's all propaganda." "Propa what?" "Political palaver laced with Buddhism and hallucinogens." "Right!" "God? I don't need a God. We're all God. We just don't realize our God-ness." "If we're all God how come we don't know it?" "Did you ever practice the *I Ching* or hyperventilate? It's the same thing." "God? I thought She was everywhere." "Look baby, I got my own way of escaping reality," said a young man showing his needle-scarred arm. "LSD makes your personality expand." Bill Cosby retorted, "Yeah, what if you're an asshole?" "You never read Aldous Huxley on peyote, or quantum physics on nothing." A woman said, "You should know the benefits of Zen brown rice on physics and primitive cultures. This world would be better off it were run by vegan women instead of meat-eating men, the hairy bastards." Another theory: "The social application of grassroots revolution is going to happen only when we completely change the definitions of all words. Words are the enemy." "What then must we do?" "Dictionaries were written by men before there was acid." "I'm completely against words. Don't get me wrong, but I like your point about grass." A man at a chess table turned to her and said, "I love you."

Some joined the General Strike for Peace, a group that would put an end to war and work. Some joined Ban the Bomb, which would put an end to nuclear holocaust. And some joined Jonathan Leek's Revolution '66, which would put an end to everything. Nobody knew what that meant, but we suspected that Leek was either a Satanist or a CIA agent provocateur.

And they went on:

"You never tried mescaline and the teachings of the *Tibetan Book of the Dead* or Che Guevara's thoughts of the people when juxtaposed with John Paul Sartre." I broke in: "It nothing much; it give you euphoria." Others went on. "You don't know if Che Guevara ate Zen macrobiotic brown rice?" "I don't, but what if he did! That would be existential." Splivey the drummer had had enough.

"What's with the brown rice! Look, bitch, we're gonna tie you to that chair and force feed you white rice till you bust. You wanna hear the sound of one hand slappin'?" A tall young man stood up, picked up his saxophone case, and said, "Splivey, that's it!" Everyone froze. "I have now attained the great enlightenment. I am one with the universe, thank you." He left with a nauseating smile on his face.

(Others were preparing to go back to nature and live by hunting and gathering. I said, "In a couple of years they'll build a superhighway right up to your wigwam.")

And on:

"We're gonna end the bomb," Joe, the high priest of the neopagans said.

"How?"

"With the bomb. We use the system against the system. Joe retorted, "Anarchists of the world *unite!* Religion is only wishing with window dressing."

Then somebody changed the rhythm of the quibbling with a line from Zen, and slowly and gravely intoned, "The enlightened ones say, 'Those who speak do not know, and those who know do not speak.'"

I said, "Wait a minute, you just spoke that!"

"So?"

"So, that means you don't know. You wouldn't know an 'enlightened one' if he came up and grabbed you by the . . ."

"Hey baby, I'm the Pied Piper. I'll show you where it's at."

"Where what's at? I want to know what *is!*"

"What's *it* got to do with it?"

"We're not getting anywhere. This is starting to sound like Who's on First."

"'Cause you don't know where it's at, Jack."
"Where what's at? We're spiraling into chaos."
"Yeah, ain't it great!"

"Believe not because your forefathers have believed for generations. Believe not because all of society says so. Believe not because someone produces an ancient manuscript. Believe when it satisfies you logically in all ways."—quotation attributed to the Buddha

The Dilemma

Part One, Western: "Religion has convinced people that there's an invisible man living in the sky who watches everything you do every minute of every day. And the invisible man has a list of ten specific things he doesn't want you to do. And if you do any of these things, he will send you to a special place of burning and fire and smoke and torture and anguish for you to live forever, and suffer, and suffer and burn, and scream, until the end of time. But he loves you. He loves you. He loves you and he needs money. He's all powerful . . . just can't handle money."—George Carlin

Part Two, Eastern: "Hollowed out clay makes a pot, but the useful part of the pot is the part that is void."—Lao Tzu

"Brahman (the Absolute) is real; the world is false. The self and God are one." "Everything is God." "I am Brahman." "I am That."
—Shankar Acharya

The western sub-modality was: Matter is evil. Why not exploit, pollute, and go on enjoying? The eastern: If the material world is false and we are all one with God and the universe, let's go on enjoying, exploiting, and polluting.

Opiates could be had on any street corner in the '60s. The war on drugs meant arresting a few jazz musicians and one comic, Lenny Bruce. J. Edgar Hoover boasted, "There is no such thing as organized crime."

"There is no history; there are only historians."

—said by some guy I used to know

Follow the music. In the nineteenth century the waltz was banned for being too licentious. In the 1960s, popular songs went from "Kumbayah" to "Blowin' in the Wind" to "We Gotta Get Out of This Place," and then descended to "Eve of Destruction," "Paint it Black," and finally the Fugs:

> Monday, nothing
> Tuesday, nothing
> Wednesday and Thursday, nothing
> Friday, for a change
> a little more nothing
> Saturday, once more nothing

One evening Tiny Tim was performing in the back room of the Rienzi Café. The audience of fifty to sixty people giggled incessantly. I sat with Ryder, an intellectual who always carried a laundry sack full of books. He handed me a slip of paper about an inch and a half long, ragged on the edges, like parchment. It had a blue-green spot stain in the middle.

"This is Owsley acid," he said. "Five bucks."

"Sure."

"Do not take the whole thing!" he said emphatically. "Cut it in half, swallow it, and give the other half to a friend."

"I plan to take it and do yoga." I said.

"You know, I do yoga too. There's this swami on the Lower East Side who's chanting."

"Really!" I said. "Where?"

"At 26 Second Avenue, around First Street."

"What is he chanting?"

"Hare Krishna, Hare Krishna, Krishna Krishna, Hare Hare/ Hare Rama, Hare Rama, Rama Rama, Hare Hare."

"Oh," I said, "I never heard of that before."

"He's very different, this swami. He'll propose a question, and people will start debating and arguing between themselves, and he just sits back and lets them talk. And then he answers the question."

One way to take the teeth out of a revolution is to make it fashionable. Greenwich Village changed when The Lovin' Spoonful played at the Night Owl Cafe and brought on the rock 'n' roll scene. Macdougal Street had now gone commercial. Rock 'n' roll was more profitable than Beat poetry and folk music. On the east side of the fountain in Washington Square Park there is a statue of the Italian hero, Garibaldi, with his hand on the hilt of his sword. Tour guides explain that if a virgin should walk under the stature, he will draw his sword; in over a hundred years he never has. We resented that New York University called Washington Square Park their campus.

"This is a public park!" we said.

That led to a whole lot of wrangling and angry words about

what instruments could be played.

"No drums," NYU said, "only stringed instruments. Drums are disturbing the classes."

Some groups wanted to protest New York University with a parade and a march, and others, of the Che Guevara system, wanted to pick up a gun.

A young bearded fellow in jeans, a beret, and various military clothes of no known army said, "Che told me, 'If you aren't willing to pick up a gun to support your beliefs, then it's just middle class rhetoric.'"

The drumming in Washington Square was banned, but not the bomb.

We'd hear, "There's going to be a big bust." That was going on all the time; everybody was afraid of an arrest. Or they didn't care. Euphoria is the side effect of drugs, but the main effect is that you just don't give a damn about anything.

I was invited to a party at a rich friend's apartment. There were about twenty seekers of absolute and relative truths drinking, smoking, playing records by Bob Dylan, The Rolling Stones, Ravi Shankar. A twenty-two-year-old beauty wearing a sheer paisley blouse and no bra sat next to me on the couch. She had the body of a six-foot-tall Radio City Rockette (she was one).

I said, "I'm looking for a chick."

"So am I," she said.

Later on, the host passed out LSD sugar cubes. I had kept my piece of paper at home. Everybody expected an orgy, but the more the acid moved me, the less I was interested in anything physical. Everybody on acid sees vivid colors, but I saw the refraction of colors that came from every light, and then every shadow, and then they multiplied exponentially. There are no withdrawal symptoms from

LSD because the effects never go away. The next morning, I saw the clouds in the sky edged in spectral colors, floating rainbows. It was the sunlight refracted through the water vapors—Hmm, rather fine.

Once upon a time the sun god asked some of his servants, the sun rays, "Go find and bring back some shadows."

The sunrays returned and said, "We have no shadows for you. Everywhere we went the shadows ran away and disappeared."

About a week or two later, the party was at my mom's house while she was away. My friends and seekers of both absolute and relative truths came. I put half the Owsley paper on my tongue. The Rockette was writhing on the floor. I saw the flickering lights and the rainbows. A paisley Persian blouse pattern was moving on the bare white ceiling.

Then there was a change. I had a vision of a fixed field of deep brown with azure concentric circles as fine as grooves on a record. I knew something very important was happening and had to be experienced in private. How am I going to get everyone out? The phone rang. It was Splivey.

"Hey, I heard you're having a party, man. Can I come over?"

"No! No! It's unbearable! They won't leave! I can't stand it!"

"Okay, I won't add to your burden."

"Thank you, Splivey."

"Okay, everybody out! Yah don't have to go home, but you can't stay here."

They left. I was alone now. I took out my meditation carpet, got into a lotus position, vibrated a few long *oms,* straightened out my spine, my bones, my senses. And then it exploded.

The *ajna chakra* is a lotus of only two petals, situated between the eyes. A form in the shape and colors of two peacock feathers joined horizontally by their shafts expanded within my closed eyes. The shafts were bound with flaming cords. The spectral-colored shapes in the feathers moved outward from the center, left and right like two animated rainbows, wave after wave, as bright as the sun. Nothing else existed. After ten to twelve minutes it faded. I was still sitting in the lotus position, and that was the position I was in when I woke up six hours later.

Actually I was only seeing the backs of my retinas. But who or what was doing the seeing?

The sun was out. *Yes, the sun,* I thought. *We're living in a mandala: the solar system. The sun, the center, sends light into planets and clouds. Some powerful mandala that sun creates. I'm a little speck walking around on a planet within it. Yes, I'm still in this world. Damn it! This is a New York apartment, not liberation. I need a guide. What do I do with this experience? Put it on a resume? "High school grad, plays flute, some typing, sees chakras."*

I remembered what Ryder had told me about the swami who chants Hare Krishna at 26 Second Avenue. That evening I started off for the swami's place.

two

26 Second Avenue:
The Storefront Monastery

In 1966 the Lower East Side of New York City was not fashionable. It was a neighborhood of bleak warehouses and sweatshops that reminded me that most people work nine-to-five jobs. Nobody went there at night. I had always walked west to Macdougal Street and beyond. Everything hip was west. This evening I walked east. The streets were empty except for a few winos, who weren't threats in the days before crack. They were often talented, educated, even friendly. Some were great poets; some were former university professors, or even former senators. I passed one sitting in a doorway.

"Kind sir," he said gently, "I seem to be short-funded. A loan of only seventeen cents is all I need for some wine."

"I don't have seventeen cents."

If he'd asked for a quarter I would have given him one. I walked on past him and looked back to check that he wasn't following me.

He shouted after me pathetically, "Why do you look back in disdain?"

Was he an "enlightened one" in disguise? I better see what this swami's like first.

I arrived at 26 Second Avenue and looked in the window. It had been a small store, about fifteen feet wide and twenty feet to the back wall. From within I heard brass cymbals clanging in a one-two-three beat. Above the front window was a sign, MATCHLESS GIFTS. The former business sold scented candles, incense, and probably matches. It was all gutted and cleared out now. Nothing significant had ever happened in this store. If those walls could talk we'd be bored to death. A black spot on the linoleum floor was once a piece of bubble gum, now a permanent fossil. In the window were three brick-colored hardbound books and a typewritten notecard scotch-taped to the glass that read "Srimad Bhagavatam Translated from the original Sanskrit with elaborate commentary by A. C. Bhaktivedanta Swami." I was intrigued that the word Vedanta was in his title.[1] A young couple standing next to me was also looking in the window. We could hear the muffled sound of hand cymbals and drums.

I joined my palms together and asked them, "Is this 26 Second Avenue?"

Giggling, they said, "Pilgrim, your search has ended," and walked away.

I went into the store. Sitting on the bare floor were about twenty-five young men and women, some playing hand cymbals, and all chanting the Hare Krishna mantra. One fellow looked like a Hebraic Paul Bunyan in overalls. A woman was dressed modestly, and one gentleman looked like a conservative accountant (he was one). I sat

in my most perfect lotus posture and joined in the chanting: Hare
Krishna, Hare Krishna, Krishna Krishna, Hare Hare/ Hare Rama,
Hare Rama, Rama Rama, Hare Hare.

At the far end, seated on a straw mat on the floor, playing hand
cymbals and chanting Hare Krishna, was A. C. Bhaktivedanta Swami. His head and face were shaved, and the simple saffron robes he

---

1 Sripad Bhaktisiddhanta, the founder of the Gaudiya mission, had a one-
man governing body commissioner, a real "son of the mother." When Bhaktisiddhanta was alive, this disciple had managed all the properties and assets of
the mission, making a good living for himself. Some of his other disciples com-
plained to Bhaktisiddhanta that this manager was amassing money. Prabhupada
told me that Bhaktisiddhanta said, "If we had to hire a manager it would cost
ten times what he is taking, and if there are any more complaints I will declare
him my successor today."

After the passing of Bhaktisiddhanta in 1936, this manager had the birthplace of Lord Chaitanya and other important temples sequestered to him by
a private trust that excluded all the other missionaries. When the leading missionary, Bhakti Prajnan Keshava Maharaj, came to the birthplace temple, the
manager ordered him out. Keshava Swami began court cases to recover the properties, but the manager's brother and son were London-educated barristers. He
had planned this decades earlier. There would be no chance of any Indian attor-
ney defeating them in court during the British Raj.

This fighting went on for several years, and Keshava Maharaj and others
had a council with their godbrother, Swami Bhakti Rakshak Sridhar, another of
the leading missionaries. He advised them to cease litigations and begin their
own ashrams. Keshava Swami privately consulted with Sridhar about his plan to
establish an order of *sannyasis,* all having the name "Bhaktisiddhanta." Sridhar
Maharaj said that since that is the name of their guru, they should think of
something else. They decided on the title Bhaktivedanta.

Bhakti-siddhanta can mean "devotional principles," and *bhakti-vedanta*
means "attaining the conclusion of the *Vedas* by devotional service." The aca-
demic world, yoga societies, the Vedanta Society—all used the esoteric term
vedanta. Prabhupada's having Vedanta in his name had far more impact, all due
to a conversation between two swamis on a minor point of etiquette over twenty
years before.

wore were not hemmed but torn off at the edges. On his forehead and nose was a pale yellow mark of two vertical lines that extended from between his brows to his hairline. I thought this must allude to his third eye or his *ajna chakra*. His eyes were closed in concentration, and he looked like he had the wisdom of the prime minister of the galaxy.

The chanting, or *sankirtan,* lasted for another ten minutes; then the swami solemnly recited some Sanskrit prayers and began his talk. His seventy-year-old voice had the tone and timbre of a cello.

Thank you, boys and girls, for coming. It is very nice that you have come here to hear the chanting of this Hare Krishna *maha-mantra*. God is nondifferent from His name, form, qualities, and pastimes. This *maha-mantra* is nondifferent from Krishna Himself.

We are all wandering in this material world, taking birth in eight million four hundred thousand species of life, animal or human or demigod. We have taken bodies of various kinds. This human form of life is the best opportunity for God realization. Now we can understand we are not this American body but pure spirit soul. We must give up all identification with the body and all the designations that accompany it: "I am American." "I am Indian." "I am white." "I am black."

The great sage Narada Muni says, *sarvopadi vinir muktam. Mukti* means liberation—liberated from all these bodily designations. You are thinking, "I am American, Indian, or Japanese. I am white or black, young or old." These are all bodily conceptions of life. It is temporary illusion. I have seen in front of your United Nations building, and there are so many flags. When there will be one flag, then you can say the world is united. If there is to be a brotherhood of man, there must be a fatherhood of God. Just as the material body has a spirit soul, so the whole material creation has a soul. That is Krishna. The chanting of Hare Krishna cleanses the mirror of the mind. So long as our consciousness is dirty, no plans for world peace or any peace is possible.

After his talk he cut up an orange, and a bearded disciple, who looked like Jesus in jeans, passed the pieces around on a plate. I leaned towards a bearded, longhaired man in black jeans.

"Well, that solves the world's problems."

"Yeah," he said," and that's just the beginning."

"You know the Swami?"

"I've been coming for a few months."

He was professor Howard Wheeler, later initiated as Hayagriva. No intellectual slouch, at age twenty-eight he was the youngest professor of English to hold tenure at the University of North Carolina.

The Swami (at this time the title Prabhupada had not been adopted) left through a side door. I went home. I wanted to meet the Swami in private. I would tell him about my yoga experiences. It must be difficult for a seventy-year-old holy man living alone in New York. Maybe I could help him. It might be a nice supplement to my yoga practice. I didn't know how naïve my ambitions were.

A few days later I moved out of my mother's place into a typical one-bedroom railroad apartment on Avenue A and Eighteenth Street. It wasn't so bad, even if it had rats and roaches. The bathtub was in the kitchen.

I went to the temple every week. On one visit, after we chanted Hare Krishna, the Swami explained how chanting is as natural as a young baby's crying for its mother's love. Then the *sankirtan* started again. We went beyond the meditative mood and the sound we had previously intoned, like the monotonic basso profundo of the Tibetan monks or Gregorian chants. This time we wailed! Hands in the air! People outside the window peeked into the room, mouths open, thinking something had happened, something good, or somebody did something great. Somebody did. And then the Swami stood up, raised his arms, and swayed along with us.

Amidst the chanting and the clanging of cymbals, I asked Professor Howard, chanting and swaying next to me, "Are we ever going to sit with the Swami and meditate?"

He leaned over and said, "Never trust a holy man who can't dance."

Time did not matter; nothing else mattered except Hare Krishna chanting. We were melting into the mantra, and we were raising the roof.

After the *kirtan* a guest told me, "I was bathed in light, bathed in light!"

"Once when I was chanting," another said, "I got goose bumps and my hair just stood on end."

When the chanting ended, the Swami took out a plate of sweets.

"Look what I have made," he said, and passed out the sweets.

I leaned over to Howard and said, "Never trust a holy man who can't cook either."

Afterwards I asked "Jesus," "Can I go up and speak to the Swami?"

"Yeah, sure."

Two or three other men came with me. Behind the store was a little garden. Past that was the five-story apartment building where the Swami lived. We entered his rooms on the second floor.

On the left was a room with a parquet floor and his altar, made from a small table. On the marble-topped table was a brass incense holder, and beside it, a small brass hand bell. A picture of Krishna and a picture of five unusual-looking figures were the centerpiece. (Indian illustrators disregard human anatomy proportions when painting divine beings.) The five standing figures were Chaitanya (the fifteenth-century incarnation of Krishna) and his four main associates. Their arms were raised in praise, and they had deep, dreamy-yet-serious stares in their eyes. I knew I would have a lot of questions.

I sat with a few others in the room adjoining the one where the Swami held court. He sat cross-legged on a folded brown woolen blanket on the floor behind a metal box that served as both a low desk and a storage box. His typewriter rested on the floor next to him, and dozens of the brick-colored books filled each corner.

I didn't hear what a woman had asked, but the Swami was saying, "This is lack of knowledge."

Then he handed her a copy of the *Gita*. Until his own translation came out, he used the Dr. Radhakrishnan edition. He said the commentary was imperfect but the verse translations were all right. Whenever anyone asked a question, he would hand them the book and tell them to go to this or that chapter and verse and read. This demonstrated that his answers were based on the *Gita* and not his own ideas or speculations. He was passing down the explanations from Krishna directly.

"At night, can you find the sun?" he asked the woman. "Even with a hundred-power flashlight you cannot see the sun, and when the sun is in the sky, what is the use of your flashlight?"

"But there are so many phonies," the woman said. "How do I know what to believe in?"

The Swami answered, "It is like trading counterfeit coins: If there is counterfeit, that means there must be real money. Similarly, if there is imitation, there must be the genuine thing. We have the Vedic literature, the character of *sadhus* from time immemorial, and the present guide. Sadhu, *shastra* [Vedic scripture], guru. These three are the method for proof; then you apply your own intelligence with your own direct experience."

"So why are there so many different religions? Which one is real?"

"You have the pocket dictionary," he replied, "and the ten-thousand-page dictionary. The pocket edition is not wrong, but the library edition is more complete."

Then it was my turn.

"Can you teach me *raja*-yoga?"

The *raja*-yoga, *hatha*-yoga, and *ashtanga*-yoga systems lead to *samadhi,* the perfect trance, which I thought I was well on my way to attaining but needed a guide. He passed me the *Bhagavad Gita*.

"Go to ninth chapter. Read from the second verse."

I read aloud, "This is the king of knowledge, the . . ."

"Stop there. *Raja*-yoga," he explained, "can mean the king of yoga or the yoga of kings. In Vedic times kings were yogis, not like your elected politicians."

We laughed.

"Now go to the sixth chapter, last verse."[2]

I read: "And of all yogis, he who always abides in Me with great

---

2 http://www.asitis.com/6/47.html

faith, worshiping Me in transcendental loving service, is most inti-
mately united with Me in yoga and is the highest of all."

"Nothing will come of nothing."—King Lear
"Everything is personal."—Michael Corleone

Raymond started to ask, "In your religion . . ."

The Swami cut him off sharply.

"This is not religion! This is knowledge."

Raymond reframed his question.

"Is everything God or made out of God? The pantheists say,
'God doesn't create the world; He becomes the world.'"

"That is all right," the Swami said, "but He remains full in the
balance. *Ishopanishad* says, *purnam-evavashishyate:* God is complete.
If you add, multiply, divide infinity, you get infinity. And if you
subtract infinity from infinity, the remainder is infinity."

Then Raymond asked, "What is the Absolute Truth?"

The Swami answered without moving a muscle: "That which
is!"

Then he said it emphatically in Sanskrit: *"Evam tattva vidas tat-
tvam.* 'The really real thing.' It is repetitious for emphasis."

Someone else asked, "Don't we all become one with God?"

"Nothing is separate from God; that's all right. We are one in
quality with God, but we do not become God."

The Swami pretended to lick his hand and said, "It is like saying I am salty, so I am the ocean. This version is inadequate and defective. The potency is nondifferent from the potent. The energy is
nondifferent from the energetic. The effective, immediate, and in-
gredient causes cannot be less than the result. Yes?"

We sat silent, impressed with the answer and the extent of the swami's vocabulary.

Seeing us hesitate, he said, "You want it in simple language?"

We all nodded.

"If I see you, I see your father. Were any of your ancestors a formless energy?"

Then he confirmed, "If it cannot be said in simple language, it is bogus."

"Then, who is Krishna?"

"Krishna is the original cause of all causes."

That hung in the air for a while. Until another one of us asked, "But aren't we all the same, all one?"

The Swami cut in, "The impersonalists have this example: God is like the all-pervasive air. If you have a pot, the air takes the shape of the pot. Break the pot and the air in the pot merges with the all-pervasive air. This is called 'big air' and 'little air.' It is a very cunning argument. You agree?"

We all agreed, having heard that version before.

But then he retorted, "Yes, but an analogy has to have some similarity with the thing being described. The analogy that has the most similarities is the best. First of all, the spirit soul and God are nothing like air. It is described in the *Upanishads* as like a spark of sunshine and the sun. Sunshine is all-pervasive, but can a spark of sunshine become the sun?"

We were silent.

"Just answer. Can a spark of sun become the whole sun planet?"

"No," we said all together.

"Again," he continued, "back to the example of air in the pot. If everything is only formless void, then who made the pot? Where does this nonsense pot come from? It is simply jugglery of words."

Someone said, "It's all God's dream."

"That is another nonsense. Just try to understand. A formless impersonal void cannot dream of pots!"

We had no response. We agreed. That's called teaching.

I came one evening and got to speak to the Swami alone. He was typing furiously with two fingers.

"Yes, come on," he said.

Professor Howard was sitting with the Swami and boldly said, "I'm going to renounce the world."

The Swami paused and said calmly, "You do not own the world, so how can you renounce it?"

Professor Howard considered that and smiled.

The Swami continued, "Everything belongs to Krishna, not us. Knowing that is renunciation."

Howard bowed and left me alone with the Swami.

I asked, "There are two verses in the *Gita* I don't understand but know contain the answer to something."

Stumbling on the words, I asked if he knew their meaning. I paraphrased: "All beings are in Me, but I am not in them. Yet everything does not rest in Me. Behold My mystic potency."

"It's fabulous," I said, "but inconceivable. How is Krishna in everything and not . . . ?

He gestured me to stop, handed me the *Gita,* and said, "Just read from chapter nine, verses four and five."

He quoted the verses himself: "By Me, all these worlds are pervaded. All beings are in Me, but I am not in them. And yet all that is created does not rest in Me. Behold My mystic opulence!"

"Yes, those two," I said. "But how can Krishna be everywhere?

How can God have a form and also be everywhere? If He is all-pervading, He must be formless."

"Again just like the sun," the Swami replied. "The sun has a form and from this form spreads light and heat everywhere. The light and heat cannot be separated from the sun. Can you say there is sun without light and heat?"

"No," I said, "but isn't Krishna in me?"

"Yes," he replied confidently. "Just like if you have many pots of water, you can see the sun disc reflected in each one, but the sun planet is far away in the sky. You understand?"

"Yes."

But I went on pressing my question.

"Then Krishna says, 'Everything is in Me.' I don't understand. He's in and out, not in, not out?"

He continued, "Krishna says in the *Bhagavad Gita,* 'I first taught this science to Vivaswan.' That is the name of the sun god. So the sun represents Krishna in so many ways. The tree is a product of sunlight, yes? By photo . . . how do you say?"

"Photosynthesis."

"Thank you. A tree is nothing but transformation of sunlight. All vegetation is a product of the external energy of the sun far, far away from the sun planet. When you think of the sun, there is the sun planet, the sun disc, the sun's heat and light, and all the properties of sunlight to make life on this earth. Still, there is no tree in the sun. It would burn up, yes?"

"Yes."

"The tree is the byproduct of the sun's external energy, but sitting under the tree, can you get a sunburn? Just say."

"No," I answered.

"Very good. Under the tree is shade. When you touch a tree it is not hot. But within the sun are all the properties to create the tree. Dormant sun energy is stored as wood in the tree; make heat by friction, and the sun energy comes out as fire. Sunlight evaporates ocean water to make the cloud to feed the tree water. Then sometimes the cloud produces lightning and sets the tree on fire. So when you see all the trees in this world, you are seeing the influence of the sun. But in the sun planet there is no water or cloud. Can the tree create the sun? Certainly not. Similarly everything we see is the influence of Krishna, but it is not Krishna Himself. Like this, God can exist in His own abode and simultaneously be the all-pervasive controller of the universe. This is *bhakti*-yoga, Krishna consciousness."

"Now I understand."

His examples covered every angle. I paid my respects and left.

As I got to the door, he said to me, "Thank you very much. I appreciate this question," and went back to his typewriter.

I left through the now-dark storefront and stood out on Second Avenue. I looked around and saw the bleak neighborhood, the shabby auto garage next to the store. Across the avenue was a broken-down car, stripped by mechanics or thieves.

I thought, *Do you know what just happened in there? Do you know what he just did? He gave me the answers to the most cosmic, theological, universal, eternal questions ever asked! And like it was just matter-of-fact! Then he thanks me for asking! I gotta tell people about this.*

On the order of his spiritual master, Srila Prabhupada had come to the USA on a steamship from Calcutta at age seventy. He once told me that early in his New York days he had to share a room with a hippie couple. "I had to keep my food next to their meat in the refrigerator. They were not clean. I slept in the bed next to theirs.

And sometimes they were not sleeping."

He kept diary entries of his daily expenditures. One January 1966 entry reads, "Went to Brentano bookstore and returned to 72nd Street apartment. Bus fare, fifteen cents." That meant he walked one way in the snow. He tore used envelopes inside-out for his notepapers. In the eighteenth century a great-grandsire of the Krishna movement, Vishwanath Chakravarti, wrote, "Difficulties in preaching are a thousand times more powerful than performances of austerities." Pious fasting and severe penances are planned, but as any boxer will tell you, "The punch that hurts the most is the one you don't see coming." I defy any yogi or sage from the glorious ancient times to perform an austerity as difficult as living with two stoned hippies in the Bowery in the winter of 1966.

On another evening after the *kirtan,* a few of us went up to see the Swami.

"Yes, come on," he said.

Someone asked, "But isn't everything God?"

"Matter is matter; spirit is spirit," he replied. "Material creation is called God because it is God's energy. Electricity is hot by nature, but when it runs the refrigerator, the effect is cold. Just like we have a body, and consciousness is spread all over the body. However, we have hair and nails that are not alive. You can cut them. There is no pain. There is no feeling. But if you see some fingernail on the ground, you know it came from somebody's hand. In the spiritual sky there is only consciousness in ecstasy for eternity. In this world everything is different from each other thing. If you say 'water, water,' it is not water. In Vaikuntha, the spiritual world, everything, even an inanimate thing, is Krishna's conscious servant. For example, He does not have to ask for a chair; when He wants to sit down,

His chair comes. When we chant Krishna, He is here."

Someone asked, "You said that we souls have been transmigrating birth after birth in the material world from time immemorial, so how and when did we fall into illusion?"

The Swami asked, "Did you go to sleep last night?"

"Yes."

"What time was it?"

"Well, I think . . ."

"You were unconscious; therefore you do not know exactly when you fell asleep. When you reawaken, then it will not matter. The original condition of water is liquid. Ice may be frozen for millions of years, but as soon as you bring heat, it is liquid again. The natural state of the soul is Krishna consciousness, but the soul wants to enjoy separate from Krishna, so there is this material world for Krishna unconsciousness. Chanting Hare Krishna awakens our dormant, natural. constitutional spiritual state."

Another question: "Why does it say in some *Vedanta* books 'We are God?'"

The Swami responded, "The *Upanishad* says, 'He has hands and feet everywhere.' Look at your hand. Everything belongs to God, yes?"

"Yes."

"Then your hand also belongs to God. So you can say this is God's hand. But your hand is not all-powerful like Krishna's. Still, the same example of the hand: If the hand is amputated it cannot function. When the hand is attached, it functions. But you don't say 'I hand'; you say 'my hand.' When it functions to serve your sense enjoyment, it is amputated from God, but when used in Krishna's purpose, it is acting for Krishna. Then it is one of His hands. Now your hand is Krishna's hand. Krishna has unlimited hands, and He likes to use all His hands for Himself, for His own enjoyment, just like you like to use yours for your enjoyment. So why not use it for Krishna? Similarly, all this is Krishna's energy, but it does not act like spirit. By putting an iron rod into the fire it becomes hot. When it becomes red-hot it then acts like fire."

I asked, "Where did you live in India?"

"Vrindavan."

"What is it like?"

"Oh, you can become more Krishna conscious in one day in Vrindavan than ten years in America."

It was after eleven o'clock at night, and yet this seventy-year-old holy man said, "You are all tired. I will stop?"

"No, go on, go on."

"Any more question? I will go all night!"

A young woman asked, "How can God allow all this suffering and war?"

The Swami replied, "At night, when the sun is set, the thieves do their business. Is it the fault of the sun? And when the sun rises, all the thieves curse the sun and run away."

"I see," she said,

"Any more question?"

"You're really helping us understand," someone said.

"By associating with you," he said, "it is enriching my Krishna consciousness."

We thanked him genuinely for that blessing.

He still showed no sign of drowsiness, but we bowed and left. We weren't drowsy either, but we had a lot to absorb.

And soon after the roof caved in, literally.

One evening I was at home reading my Theosophical Society edition of the *Bhagavad Gita,* and a few chips of plaster fell on the pages. I looked up and saw three huge cracks moving into the center of the ceiling. Three two-inch-thick chunks of plaster were sagging and ready to fall. I got out of the room to look for somebody like a building superintendent, but there was none. As soon as I got to the ground floor I heard a sound as if a shotgun went off. I went back upstairs and saw a cloud of dust. The pieces of plaster, each about a yard wide and two inches thick, had smashed everything in my room.

I went to 26 Second Avenue. It was early evening, about seven o'clock. I told Swamiji what happened.

"Krishna saved you," he said.

"Can I sleep here tonight?"

"Yes, just go downstairs. The boys will help you."

One of the "boys" was Bruce, later Brahmananda, the Hebrew Paul Bunyan. The Swami called him "the mountain of our mission." He wore work pants, a T-shirt, and red suspenders. The other "boy" was Keith, later Kirtanananda, the son of a Baptist pastor at an affluent Long Island church. He seemed to know every line of the Bible.

Bruce's brother Gregory (later Gargamuni) lived in the store as well.

"We'll put some blankets down here and there," he said. "We have rats."

Bruce had met the Swami a few months before and had called his brother in Arizona.

"I've found it!"

"Found what?"

"The real thing! Come to New York."

In a recent lecture, the Swami told us the story of a cruel hunter who shot animals "and left them flapping." We were amused by the Swami's word "flapping." The story goes on to tell how Narada, a great sage, told the hunter, "Don't leave them flapping. At least kill them quickly." By the association of the sage, the hunter gave up all killing, not even stepping on ants, and became a devotee of Krishna.

I slept in the store with the boys that night. We heard the skittering of the rats. Brahmananda tossed around, bolted up, and turned on a light. No rats. It was Gargamuni tickling him.

Gargamuni was laughing. "You were flapping."

The Swami said we could shower in his bathroom, so the next morning, the four of us, along with the Swami, shared one large blue towel.

Brahmananda told me we could become initiated disciples of the Swami. That would show our seriousness in learning and practicing.

"What's involved?" I asked.

"Well, it would be better if you shaved up."

By "shaved up" he meant having my head shaved with an electric razor.

I hadn't had a haircut in over a year, but I said, "Buzz me, baby!"

He did, leaving a small, round tuft of hair in the back, known as a *sikha*. The *sikha* shows that one is a student and servant of a spiritual master and God and it distinguishes Krishna devotees from impersonalists and Buddhists, whose heads are completely shaved.

After a day or two the shock of being bald passed. It was a lot easier to dry off after a shower too, and nothing to comb.

"Now I can see your face," Brahmananda told me.

Then he explained what initiation involved: "The Swami's four rules are (1) no gambling, (2) no illicit sex, (3) no eating of meat, fish, or eggs, and (4) no intoxication. That includes smoking tobacco and even drinking coffee and tea."

"Hmm, I can do all those . . . but what was that second thing?"

"It means to either remain celibate or be married."

I thought, I'm not going to be a married man with a family and practice yoga on the weekends. I'll stick it out single.

Some days later the Swami told this story: Once a rich landlord, while inspecting his land, saw a beautiful woman living on one of his properties.

He came by and said, "You should not be laboring in my fields. I'm going to move you to my house, and you will do various services." (wink, wink)

"Yes, I will come with you," she said. "Come back in three days."

Thereafter, she took a very strong purgative, threw up, and passed liquid stool for three days. She kept the stool and vomit in three buckets.

On the third day, the landholder came back, and she was in rags, discolored, and thin.

"Where's the beautiful girl I'm here to take?"

"I am that girl."

"Oh, where is your beauty? Three days ago you were beautiful."

"There. I have kept it in the three buckets. Take them with you."

This story is called liquid beauty.

Hearing the story made me think, This is a real guru. The fashionable 'uptown' gurus who came through New York would never tell a story like that. This is old school.

I envisioned young sages sitting at their master's feet from time immemorial hearing this story. This was old, very old-time religion.

A young woman once asked the Swami, "Why do I have to worship God? Can't I be just a good person? I just worship nature."

The Swami shot back, "Whose nature?" The material scientists are absorbed in energy—atomic energy, electrical energy, and so on—but they have no knowledge of the energetic, Krishna. When you know the energetic, the energy is automatically understood in proper relation."

We asked the Swami about his prayer beads.

"Yes," he said. "These are beads on which you chant Hare Krishna. *Japa* is chanting in the mouth. When you are initiated you can also have beads."

We all bought wooden beads from a crafts store and strung them ourselves, with a knot between each bead. The *japa-mala,* or string of 108 *japa* beads, represents the 108 *gopis* (cowherd girls) who are individual divine energies of Krishna. One oversized bead marks where you finish one "round" and then go back in the opposite direction for the next round. At the initiation ceremony, the Swami would ask his new disciples to vow to chant sixteen rounds each day.

We asked him, "Why do you use a bag to hold the beads when you chant on them?"

He opened his trunk and took out a piece of cardboard shaped in an asymmetrical ellipse. It was the sewing pattern for a bead bag.

"Here. You make four sides from this."

Along with boxes of books, a tiered cooking pot, and other luggage from India, he had also remembered to pack that pattern, anticipating that westerners would take up the practice of *japa* meditation. The bag is used because the *japa-mala* is long and should not touch the floor or get tangled on anything.

We prepared for initiation. The ceremony was held in the apartment room where the Swami worshiped Radha-Krishna. The Swami had laid out the materials and paraphernalia for a fire sacrifice. On the floor he had placed a square-foot of sand on top of the metal plate he ate from. Arranged on the side were kindling wood, *ghee,* and rice grains. He made lines across the sand with colored powders: red, white, and blue. (In a London initiation ceremony a few years later, a devotee made colored lines like the Union Jack and Prabhupada said, "That is nice.") He lit the wood and spooned *ghee* onto it while chanting prayers to his guru and the other gurus in his spiritual lineage. He chanted one round of Hare Krishna mantras on each set of our beads. Initiation means passing the sound of Krishna's name from master to disciple. The Swami was giving us his mantra, and now, after hearing it from his mouth and lips, it became our mantra. He also gave us our spiritual names, mine being Achyutananda Das Brahmachari. *Das* means "servant," and a *brahmachari* is a celibate.[3]

Later I asked him the meaning of the first part of my name, the combination of two words: *achyuta* and *ananda.*

"*Achyuta,*" he explained, "is a name for Krishna meaning infalli-

---

3 The president of a major insurance company tells this story: "While attending a conference in a large hotel, I saw in the adjoining lobby a shoeshine parlor. A very old gentleman was shining my shoes. As I sat in the high chair, reading a magazine, I looked down and asked him, 'How long have you been shining shoes?' He looked up and said, 'I don't shine shoes.' I paused and asked, 'What do you do?' To which he replied, 'I extend the life of shoes.' So ladies and gentlemen, I don't want any of my reps calling themselves insurance salesmen. Pick a title for yourself that describes the benefit you provide."

ble. *Ananda* is bliss. One who takes pleasure in the quality of Krishna's infallibility never falls down."

Why he gave me that name I'll never know. Will I ever live up to it?

By meeting the Swami I received the answer to the question "Who am I?" Now I could understand myself to be simply an atom of light in the effulgent rays of the spiritual sun Sri Krishna. Although atomic by nature, I have my own inherent value, purpose, and a drop of spiritual bliss. I am a spiritual particle. Even though that spiritual form is atomic, it is like Sri Krishna's form.

After the fire sacrifice, we watched the Swami put on his *tilak*. He spooned a few drops of water from a small brass cup into his left palm and then made a thin paste with a small chunk of clay. He held a small folding mirror in the fingers of his left hand, and with his right-hand ring finger he made the mystical sign on his nose and forehead.

"This is *tilak*. I can also do it without the mirror. It is a clay from India, and we wear it to distinguish us from the monists. Their *tilak* goes horizontally."

Brahmananda's mother attended the initiation. She looked like Lauren Bacall in a trench coat. She was not amused.

"I guess I shouldn't have taken you to all those Indian movies. What do I tell everybody now, 'My son, the swami?'"

After the fire sacrifice, the Swami told Brahmananda, "Now just go and bow down to your mother."

It was hard, but we all remained serious while Brahmananda bowed down to Mrs. Scharf.

The day after the initiations, I chanted Hare Krishna to every theme, melody, and rhythm I knew. I chanted Hare Krishna in foreign accents, in a high-pitched voice, in a medium voice, in a deep voice.

Kirtanananda came down to the store from the Swami's apartment and said, "Come upstairs to the kitchen; Swamiji is cooking."

The Swami was at the stove in the small kitchen.

"You all must learn to cook. Every Indian gentleman can cook."

He had a three-tiered brass cooking pot, simple and brilliant in design and function. The bottom of the cooker was a brass pot.

"In here you put this *dahl* [split peas], water, salt, and three potatoes."

The second section fit on top of the bottom one. It had about eight half-inch round holes in the bottom to let steam rise through.

"Put that on next. In this section you put vegetables."

We put in cauliflower and some greens. The third section was also perforated.

"Up here you can put more vegetables."

Then he put a small stainless-steel container with rice and water into the top section. "Now cover it. Then turn on full flame and just let it cook." In fifteen minutes it was done. That is how a full meal of rice, *dahl,* and veggies is cooked in one step on one burner.

He taught me how to make a *chonk:* In a small iron cup he had me fry spices in *ghee* to make an essence. I put a level teaspoon of cumin, three long dry red chilies, and *hing* (asafetida).

He looked over, "Not so much *hing!*"

When the *chonk* was smoking, he pointed to a pair of long-handled tongs he'd brought from India.

"Just give me that catcher."

I handed him the tongs. He picked up the hot cup and dropped the smoking spices, along with the cup, into the *dahl.* Poof! Sizzle.

Kirtanananda and I cooked lunch daily in four big pots. The caustic smell of the chonk got us into trouble with neighbors, but the spiced *dahl* tasted great. We made brown rice for the health-food folks and fine white rice for the Swami. He showed me how to make whole-wheat *chapattis,* or *rotis.*

"Make the dough as firm as this," he said, tugging on my earlobe.

The loose flour messed up the stove, but the lathered-in-*ghee* rotis were so good.

I asked, "Why don't we eat onions and garlic? They're vegetables too."

The Swami said, "Krishna does not like. We are not so much vegetarians; we are Krishnatarians."

A few days after my lesson, I cooked my first full lunch by myself.

Swamiji was typing when I came into his room and said, "It's ready."

He looked over everything and said, "I will now offer."

I made up the one metal plate we had, and he placed it on his altar. Sitting on a mat, his left side towards the pictures of the Deities, he made slow circles with incense in his right hand while ringing a bell in his left. He chanted Sanskrit prayers in his deep, sacred voice.

"How do we offer our food to Krishna?" I asked.

"There are prayers and ritual forms, but most important is to offer with your love. Krishna is fully satisfied in Himself. He does not need our food. He wants to see our love."

It was extraordinary that in every lecture the Swami seemed to cover every point of the philosophy of Krishna consciousness. As I read the three volumes of his translation and commentaries of the *Srimad Bhagavatam,* I noticed the same phenomenon. I can say that if you took the covers off any three or four volumes of any of Srila Prabhupada's books, shuffled the pages and took any three or four pages of commentary at random, you'd get a complete overview of every principle. In a time when everything cultural was a rehash of existing art, music, and drama, originality was a rare and valued quality. The Swami wasn't imitating anyone. He was an original. And the *maha-mantra* he'd given us was fresh and original too. No matter how much we chanted it, it never grew stale, even though it is composed of only three words. The mantra is Krishna Himself, and although He is the oldest, He is ever new.

One day, after we'd all been in the store/temple discussing everything we had each heard from the Swami, he asked, "Where were you all?"

"We were downstairs discussing."

"Yes, this is called *ishtha goshti;* all sit together like family and talk about Krishna. This is nice."

Another time, the Swami told Brahmananda, "Now that we are having regular classes and serving food, we must have one signboard with letters and numbers so we can announce the days and times of the classes."

Brahmananda went out to the store and came back an hour later, frustrated and without a signboard.

"Swamiji, signboards are fifty-five dollars. We don't even have money for the rent, and . . ."

"We must have one signboard!"

Brahmananda went out again and came back with a signboard, the kind with black felt and movable plastic letters and numbers,

and put it in the window. It had the Hare Krishna *maha-mantra* and
the times of the morning and evening classes. That evening seventy-
five people came. I passed a basket around, and it came back full of
money.

It may have been a storefront, a garden, and an apartment on
the Lower East Side, but to us it might as well have been a fifteenth-
century monastery.

The only woman who came regularly was Judy, later Jadurani
(now Shyamarani). She was an artist. Her paintings were a little
crude at first, but as she heard the Swami's descriptions of Krishna's
truths and potencies, she became a skilled artist. She had also studied folk music, and one day she came with Reverend Gary Davis,
the blind pastor and gospel singer. We all sat together with the
Swami.

In an old-time baritone Southern Baptist preacher voice, the
reverend asked the Swami, "What is it that we should ask from
God?"

"We should ask for his love."

There was peaceful silence.

When Jadurani was working on a large picture of Vishnu, she
took a break to ask the Swami a question. She stood at the Swami's
door.

"Come on," he said.

She asked the Swami, "You have said that the Paramatma, the
Supersoul who lives within the heart, is 'seated' in our hearts. So is
He in a sitting position or a standing position?"

"Oh!" he replied. "That takes many thousands of lives of meditation to realize."

Disappointed, Jadurani hung her head and got up to leave, but before she got to the door, the Swami said, "He's standing."

She left very happy not to have to wait so long.

I asked the Swami, "Do we need to study the *Vedanta-sutras?*"

He answered, "The natural explanation of the *sutras* is the *Srimad Bhagavatam,* which is the description of the devotees' relationships with Krishna. In the eighteenth century, brahmins challenged our spiritual predecessor Vishwanath Chakravarti that the followers of Chaitanya Mahaprabhu had no commentary on *Vedanta.* You cannot be accepted as bona fide without one. Vishwanath was advanced in age, so his disciple Baladev Vidyabhushan composed the commentary called *Govinda Bhashya.* Sometime I will teach this commentary."

He smiled mischievously.

"These discussions are full of intricacies. For example, Krishna says in the *Gita,* 'I am the author and the knower of the Vedanta and the goal of the *Vedas.*' The impersonalists use all manner of jugglery of words to give their interpretation of the *sutras.* For example, any word can have many meanings, just like in your thesaurus. If you put an obscure meaning of a word into a sentence, you can make anything sound like nonsense. This is called *yad va, yad va,* which means 'this, or this, or this.' Just understand. *Veda* means knowledge, and *anta* means the conclusion, so *vedanta* is the conclusion of knowledge. Or you can say *ve* also means 'without' and *danta* means 'teeth.' So *vedanta* can mean a toothless old man. But Chaitanya Mahaprabhu explained how every word means Krishna."

The Swami went on to explain that the *Upanishads* and *Vedanta-sutra* describe Krishna in impersonal and esoteric language, just as any great man may be said to be wonderful, powerful, multi-talented, creative, opulent, and so on, without revealing his personality. This leads to the misinterpretation that God is formless. Like the President of the United States, he cannot be easily approached or known personally. The president's staffers take oaths and must be qualified to work with or even be near the President. At the same time, "the Presidency" includes the leader, his entourage, and all manner of paraphernalia. Another example: The lawyer says to the judge, "May it please the court." The judge is a man and the entire court simultaneously. The judge is also called "the bench." Is a judge a bench? No. When the lawyer puts something "to the bench," does it just stay on the judge's desk? No, it means it will be read by the judge.

On another topic, Prabhupada told this story:

Once, a mouse came to a mystic yogi and said, "The cats are always chasing me."

"What do you want?"

"Make me a cat."

Poof! The mouse turned into a cat.

A few days later the cat came to the yogi and said, "Now the dogs are chasing me. Make me a dog."

Poof! "You are a dog."

A few days later the dog came back and said, "Now men are kicking me in the streets and hitting me with their canes."

The guru asked, "So now you want to be a man?"

"No, make me a tiger."

Poof! He made him a tiger, and the first thing the tiger did was leap to attack the guru, and—poof!—the guru turned him back into a mouse.

If you try to overstep the authority, you again become a mouse. Everyone, even the yogis, wants liberation without serving Krishna.

They may get some reward, but again and again they fall into the material energy after some time.

Perverted Reflections

Someone asked the Swami a challenging question.

"If you say you have full knowledge, then how many windows are in the Empire State Building?"

The Swami challenged back, "How many drops of water are in a mirage?"

One day I asked, "There's a saying, 'God is real and matter is false.' Is that true?"

The Swami replied, "This is a famous slogan from the impersonalist Shankar Acharya. *Brahman satyam jagan mithya, jivo brahmanaiva naparah.* Shankar came to revive the *Vedas* after centuries of Buddhism. Buddha rejected the *Vedas* to stop animal sacrifice by preaching *ahimsa,* nonviolence. If not for Shankar, Vedic culture would have been lost forever. One has to explain the truth according to the specific time, place, and audience. Therefore, Shankar taught the same impersonal Buddhism but quoted the *Vedas.* Shankar's example of *maya,* illusion, is 'If you see a rope in the grass and mistake it for a snake, that illusion, the snake, is false, and therefore our taking this world to be real is illusion.' This is another nonsense, a jugglery of words. The comparison is defective in so many ways. Just try to understand. The rope is real and the snake is real. Your mistaking the rope for a snake is illusion due to an imperfect conclusion by your imperfect vision. Because you have previously seen a real snake, you are taking the rope to be a snake. A child who has never seen a snake is not afraid of the rope. The material world is real but temporary. We take this world as real because we have previous memory in our hearts of the real spiritual world of Goloka Vrindavan in the spiritual sky. This world is only a shadow, a perverted reflection of Braj, or Vrindavan."

Around this time, I considered all the choices and ways to live. I arrived at this conclusion: I think I'll do whatever the Swami says for the rest of my life.

One day the Swami said, "Get twenty pounds milk. I will show you how to make *gulabjamins*."

We gathered the ingredients.

"Boil the milk till it is just ready to overflow; then add the citric acid."

The milk separated into solids and liquid, or curds and whey.

"Now drain it, rub the solids smooth, make small balls, and fry them in *ghee*."

All the curd balls broke up.

"Add a little of your cornstarch."

I don't know how he knew that cornstarch would work, but it did. After an overnight soaking in sugar syrup, the balls of curd tasted like sweet sponges exploding in your mouth. But making them was a long, tedious, and expensive process.

I Accomplish a Great Service for the Devotees and All Mankind

I invented "American *gulabjamins*" when I got an idea: Wait a minute! Powdered milk is milk solids. So we don't have to make curds from gallons of milk—we use less water and make powdered-milk dough. Then we roll 'em into balls and fry 'em.

It worked!

The Swami's rule was that cooks should not wash dishes. It is a contradiction in service. The cook will not want to use as many pots as he needs if he thinks, "I'll have to wash all these later." But we had a hard time finding helpers to do the dishes.

There were twelve of us now, and the Swami called all of us to his room.

"Everyone will take one day for dishwashing."

After some silence, someone raised a hand, "I'll do Monday."

Someone else volunteered for Tuesday. Then more silence.

The Swami raised his hand and said, "I will take Thursdays."

Three hands shot up.

After six months, more than fifty people were regularly attending morning and evening *kirtan* and lectures. Lunches and Sunday feasts were so packed we had to use the garden to accommodate everyone. We set up a dais about two feet high with a bookstand for the Swami to lecture from. He would take the high step up and then settle onto the dais.

One morning he set a thick, heavy book on the bookstand.

"This is the *Chaitanya Charitamrita*."

Most scholars would translate that as "the nectar of Chaitanya's pastimes," but the Swami translated it in practical terms.

"*Chaitanya* means 'the living force,' *charit* means 'characteristics,' and *amrita* means 'immortality.' This is the characteristics of the living force in immortality."

I regularly got up at five o'clock and made a huge pot of oatmeal for twenty people who came for breakfast before going to their jobs.

One day I was serving it out and someone said, "This cereal is too hot!"

I said, "Take a walk in the forest."

I was proud of my porridge.

One day while I was cooking, the Swami called me into his room. Stanley was talking with him. By his own choice, Stanley was fasting.

"I never say not to eat!" the Swami scolded.

"I know. I just want fifty dollars to buy a can of gasoline and set myself on fire."

The Swami turned to me.

"Call Brahmananda."

I came back with Brahmananda.

"Yes, Swamiji?" he said.

"Stanley wants fifty dollars."

"Why, Swamiji?"

"Stanley, just tell him why."

"I want to buy gasoline to set myself on fire."

We all exchanged glances.

Playing right along, Brahmananda said, "But Swamiji, we don't have fifty dollars in the treasury."

"You see?" the Swami told Stanley. "We are not having the money. Now go."

He left, and the Swami said to me, "Call his mother to come and get him."

One afternoon the Swami came into the kitchen and said, "Show me what we have."

I opened up the pantry door and said, "We have a hundred pounds of sugar, a hundred pounds of potatoes, a hundred pounds of white flour, a hundred pounds of whole-wheat flour, a hundred pounds of rice, a hundred pounds of mung *dahl*, and a hundred pounds of yellow split peas."

The Swami just nodded. I didn't know if that meant good or bad.

That evening when the Swami lectured on the *Bhagavad Gita,* he spoke about how Krishna would provide everything the devotee needs. Then the Swami—this man who looked like a golden serene Buddha—became a roaring lion.

"You come see our kitchen! You will see hundred pounds sugar, hundred pounds potato, hundred pounds rice. Hundred pounds everything! You karmis [people who work only for material benefits]! You are working so hard in your office job. Do you have hundred pounds of food? Hundred pounds rice? You do not have hundred pound anything! Just see. So don't think that if you take up spiritual life you will be poor. Krishna will provide everything. He maintains this whole universe. He will maintain you."

Brahmananda and I kvelled.

The lecture continued.

"When Krishna creates a mouth, he creates the food to feed it. Someone once asked me, 'Do life's necessities come automatically?' Very nice question. When one is fully absorbed in Krishna consciousness, Krishna provides. Otherwise one must work hard. If you are just taking and eating, you are a thief. The deer is the natural food for the tiger, but the deer does not jump into the tiger's mouth. The tiger goes hungry for days together; then Krishna provides the opportunity for the tiger to catch a deer.

"There is one story of a holy man who was raised in an ashram and had never seen a woman.

"Once, as he was begging door to door, a young woman answered.

"'Yes, take some rice for the ashram.'

"'Bless you,' said the *sadhu,* 'but what happened to you? Are you sick? Your chest is so swollen.'

"The lady went to get her father, who came to the door ready to protect his daughter from some rascal.

"'What happened to him?' the *sadhu* asked, pointing to the girl.

"'What do you mean?' asked the father.

"'His chest is all swollen.'

"'Have you ever seen a woman before?'

"'What's that?'

"'Someday my daughter will have a child. When the baby comes she will feed him milk.'

"The innocent *sadhu* was amazed.

"'Krishna provides milk just when a baby needs food? If there is a natural arrangement for this, why am I begging? Krishna will provide for me too.'

"He threw away his begging bowl and danced away, chanting Hare Krishna."

A few weeks later I went into the Swami's room and said, "The building management has sent an exterminator to kill roaches. I told him to go away because we were busy."

"Very good," he said.

A few days later I had to tell him, "They sprayed all the other apartments, and now all the roaches are coming here."

He said joyfully, "They are taking shelter of Krishna's mercy."

One afternoon Brahmananda was explaining to Swamiji the nature of western psychiatry.

"Sigmund Freud, the father of this ridiculous idea, says that everything is based on sex."

To Brahmananda's surprise the Swami said, "Yes. Everything movable and immovable in this material world is motivated by sex desire. It is the perverted reflection of the original love of God. Once Kamadev, the lord of sex desire, like your Cupid, tried to shoot Lord Shiva with his flower arrows, but he was burnt to ashes by the anger of Shiva. Then Shiva heard Kamadev's laughter.

"'Now I am invisible. I will be ten thousand times more powerful.'

"But Krishna defeated Kamadev. Kamadev became overwhelmed by concentrating on Krishna's beautiful form. Then he fainted in ecstasy. Bewilderment and fainting is called Mohan, to be overwhelmed. So this is why Krishna is called Madan Mohan.'" (Madan is a name for Kamadev.)

One day the Swami announced, "We must print books, *Back to Godhead* magazine, and posters for our events. Have some of our men get jobs in a photo-offset printing company and learn this trade. They can print our books in lieu of salary."

We printed a poster ("Stay High Forever"), his pamphlet *Who Is Crazy?*, and the magazine.

After we'd written and printed four or five issues of the magazine, we asked the Swami, "Would you write an article for *Back to Godhead* magazine?"

His answer demonstrated the principle of simultaneous oneness and difference, a central doctrine of Chaitanya's philosophy.

"Are all your articles based on what you have heard from me?"

"Yes."

"Then I write all the articles."

Now wearing yellow and saffron robes of our own, we distributed the literature on the streets. The Swami dressed me in a *dhoti*.

"This goes like this, and this part like this. Yes!"

One disciple, still influenced by monistic ideas, annoyingly kept referring to the Swami as God or Krishna. He would say, "God just told me to do this." Or when asked, "Who told you to do that?" he'd say "Krishna."

One day this disciple asked the Swami if we could ask for government welfare funds, adding that we could use the money to distribute free *prasadam,* or food offered to Krishna, which has great spiritual power.

"It is not against any of our principles," the Swami replied. "The Vedic kings would support the *sadhus.* Yes, you can try."

The disciple went to the welfare office barefoot, wearing shorts and a T-shirt. He had a shaved head and a blazing look in his eye.

The welfare agent asked, "Who told you that you could apply for welfare?"

"God!" he replied.

The agent said, "Well, you have to go over to Belleview Hospital, get a psychiatric release, and bring it back to me. You can go now. I'll let them know you're coming."

When he left the office, the agent called ahead to Belleview.

"There's a guy coming over, you can't miss him. He's in shorts, barefoot, and says he talks to God."

When the disciple walked in the door of Belleview, they kept him under observation for seventy-two hours. When we heard that, we were all shocked. Some of the devotees were lawyers, and the ACLU got involved. We got him released.

Kirtanananda brought a few of his relatives to meet the Swami. One man came with his wife. I was there with a few others, and the man was angry.

"I can chant anything" he said. "I can chant *Coca-Cola, Coca-Cola, Coca-Cola* and get the same effect."

To which the Swami said, 'No, you cannot—you will stop."

"Then I can chant *shit, shit, shit.*"

Kirtanananda shot him a nasty look, and he left.

Another time a man came into the storefront and requested a meeting with Swamiji. He seemed sober and sincere. We thought the Swami could probably touch anyone's heart. When we brought him to the Swami's room, he turned red in the face.

"Today at 2:30 P. M. Eastern Standard Time I was higher than you!"

He was burning and blazing. Brahmananda moved closer to him. We were on guard.

The Swami humbly joined his palms together and said, "Please accept my humble obeisances. Now you can go downstairs with the boys."

Brahmananda put a thick grip on his arm and led him out.

Before reaching the door, the wild man said, "I am fearless. I am God!"

The Swami called him back and said, "Do you cross the street at the green light?"

"Sure."

"Then you are afraid of death."

We led him out to the street.

When we returned, the Swami said, "Don't bring up any crazies."

We all nodded to him and to each other. At that moment we

knew that Swamiji had taught us enough to have some responsibility and was giving us our first spiritual order: To use our own discrimination, based on what we had learned, and decide "Who Is Crazy?" We were making progress.

The Village Voice and other newspapers were getting the word out that there was a swami on Second Avenue. We got invited to a huge acid-rock festival at the Fillmore East. This was the first event where the Hare Krishnas appeared dressed in *dhotis,* with shaved heads and *sikhas.* The hall was like the seventh circle of hell. A shabbily dressed girl chanted and danced while guzzling from a Chianti bottle. We chanted with Allen Ginsberg, Timothy Leary, and rock celebrities. (The Swami had said, "Any manner that people hear Hare Krishna, there is benefit.") Outside the theater was Peter Orlovsky, poet and "wife" of Allen Ginsberg.

"Hare Krishna," I said.

He looked at me and started ranting at the speed of light.

"You're comin' on lousy, baby; you're comin' on lousy, baby."

I yelled, "Oh, shaddaap!"

He cringed but kept mumbling, "You're comin' on lousy, baby."

I thought, *I don't think I should have ever taken drugs.*

During a lecture someone asked Swamiji, "Does LSD help?"

Swamiji answered, "We do not recommend."

"Well, what if it helps spiritual life?"

"Even if it helps," Swamiji replied, "we do not recommend."

"How can you say that if you haven't used it?"

"My disciples have taken, and they have given it up after chanting Hare Krishna."

Brahmananda was consulting a lawyer to help renew the Swami's soon-to-expire visa. He explained to Swamiji that one way to solve the problem was to go to Canada, stay for some months, reenter the USA, and reapply.

"That is too much botheration," Swamiji said.

Brahmananda then said, "Well, the only other way is to be married to an American citizen."

Sitting with us was a pleasant mannish woman who, along with a lady friend, had been attending classes regularly for weeks.

She said, "Well, I can marry you if it will help."

"No, no." Swamiji laughed. "I am *sannyasi*. I cannot marry. But thank you. That is nice service attitude."

Brahmananda was also working to have the society registered as a religious organization. There were many details involved.

At one point the lawyer asked, "Do any of you speak Sanskrit?"

"No, only the Swami."

"Well, you can't have a religion with only one practicing member. Did you ever hear of a rabbinical student that didn't speak Hebrew?"

That point got adjusted so we didn't all need to be ordained to be considered members. Only a president, secretary, and treasurer were needed to satisfy regulations. Finally, on July 24, 1966, the International Society for Krishna Consciousness (ISKCON) was registered.

That evening in the storefront temple, sitting on the dais, Swamiji held the documents of incorporation.

Beaming like a father over his newborn son, Swamiji said, "This International Society for Krishna Consciousness, ISKCON, is a great tool we can use to spread our Hare Krishna chanting. If it is not helpful, we can dissolve it. So we must be very careful."

It was a sobering statement. We were stepping onto the global stage. At that moment I felt I was no longer a boy.

Years later, Prabhupada illustrated by his actions the difference between the institution and the spiritual message when I and another devotee were choosing names for dozens of devotees petitioning for initiation. We consulted volumes of scriptures, the thousand names of Vishnu, the thousand names of Lakshmi, of Narayan, of Surya, the sun god. Prabhupada's custom was to select names similar to the applicant's birth name. For example, my name was Chuck, so I got the name Achyutananda, and Bruce became Brahmananda. That year we got petitions from England, Ireland, Scotland, and Wales from dozens of men named Ian and over a dozen women named Ianna and Illeana. We ran out of "I" names, even from the entire spectrum of Vedic nomenclature. I went to Prabhupada and told him the problem.

"Can we name someone ISKCON Das?"

"No!" he snapped back.

I told my godbrother that the acronym ISKCON can't be used as a divine name.

At one of the later lectures the Swami explained that Krishna's form is nondifferent from Krishna Himself and therefore worshiping the Deity is not idol worship.

"Idolatry is when you concoct an image of God by your own mental speculation," he said. "Krishna's form is not a mental concoction."

Swamiji wanted ISKCON to have Deities.

On hearing that, Bhakta Vince asked, "Oh no, like in the Catholic Church?"

"No, it is not like that," the Swami replied. "You may imagine that since God is the oldest, by now he must have grown some long beard. That's all right even if you do, but what did He look like when He was a sixteen-year-old boy? And also, He never grows old. He plays His flute and is eternally youthful, as described in the scriptures. His form is not mental concoction."

Swamiji's lectures often included the metaphor of falling back into the material illusory ocean of *maya*. He would gesture as if throwing a stone.

One day Vince got confused and yelled, "I don't get it. It's just another religion, another sectarian cult."

He stomped out of the temple.

Brahmananda and I looked at each other, and I said, "He fell back into the ocean of *maya*."

Brahmananda made the gesture of throwing a stone and said, "Bloop."

After that, every time a devotee left we'd say, "Ah, he's blooped." Or if someone was misunderstanding we'd say, "I think he's gonna bloop." Or when someone didn't show up for a few weeks, we'd say, "He's probably blooped." Bloop became our word for leaving.

Some weeks later the Swami asked, "Where's that boy Vince?"

Brahmananda said, "Oh, he blooped."

Prabhupada slowly turned to Brahmananda.

"Bloop? What is this bloop?"

Brahmananda gulped and meekly said, "Well, you've been explaining how if we do not catch onto the lotus feet of Krishna, again we will fall into the ocean of material illusion. So, like a stone falling into water, it makes that sound—bloop."

Prabhupada paused, considered the word, and said, "Well then, if he has blooped, what can be done?"

We speculated as to what knowledge, what powers, the Swami possessed because he taught us, "When you serve Krishna, you are in full consciousness. Everything numinous and phenomenal is known, and one is above the influence of the material modes of nature." Was he all-powerful? All-knowing? Is he completely unaware of his body, like someone anesthetized? Would he get sick and not know it?

One day Swamiji said, "I sent that boy Bob to go shopping days ago. Where is Bob? "

"He took the money and left," someone said. "We thought you knew."

"Unless you tell me, how can I know?" the Swami replied.

At that moment we went from awestruck admirers to dedicated disciples.

Every day he lectured at seven in the morning and seven in the evening, and all day he would type constantly with two fingers. Then there was a change. One night I walked him up to his room after the lecture, about nine o'clock. He slept in his temple/bedroom, and I slept in the other room.

During the night, I heard him calling, "Achyutananda! Achyutananda!" and I went into his room.

"Just put your hand here," he said.

He took my hand and put it on his ribcage.

"Just move up and down quickly."

I swiftly stroked his chest.

"Yes, yes."

His heart was palpitating.

"Now stop. Take rest."

He called me again a few hours later. Again, rub, rub, rub.

The next morning I ran down to Kirtanananda and Brahmananda and said, "Swamiji had heart palpitations."

We ran upstairs.

This incident changed our lives. Swamiji was still climbing up and down from the dais. He was still typing with two fingers for hours and only sleeping four hours a day. We put in steps for him to get up on the dais, we got a Dictaphone recording machine so he wouldn't have to type, and we got typists and helpers to transcribe his translation of *Bhagavatam*.

We brought him to Beth Israel Hospital on Fifteenth Street and First Avenue. That was a mistake. The doctors gave him an unnecessary and painful spinal tap as well as injections. Indian Ayurvedic treatment, to which Swamiji was accustomed, has no such violent procedures. Jadurani set up portraits of Bhaktisiddhanta (Swamiji's guru) and Bhaktivinoda Thakur (Bhakti Siddhanta's father) where he could see them. We all went up to his room, and Kirtanananda told me to massage Swamiji's feet.

Swamiji's mouth dropped open. He looked at me and said to everyone, "The picture of my Guru Maharaj and Achyutananda's face look as same."

I exploded in ecstasy.

"You will be a great preacher also."

Some devotee later said to me, "So you think you're the reincarnation of Swamiji's guru?"

I said, "No! He gave me a blessing. No, I've got to study, read, practice, and learn to preach. The Swami has also said, 'What you learn easily is easy to forget. What you learn with difficulty will be difficult to forget.'"

We all went to the hospital the next day. Swami Satchidananda came to visit and pay his respects.

When he left, Jadurani asked Swamiji, "Is he a real swami?"

Swamiji replied, "Why not?"

Then the doctor came in to examine him, and Swamiji grabbed the doctor's wrists firmly in both hands and said, "I feel all right. I want to go home."

The doctor's mouth dropped open.

"Yes, I'm going home!"

We took him back to 26 Second Avenue and started preparing for his return to India. He would be accompanied to India by Kirtanananda, and I would follow later that September. He did not want to die in a hospital, where the only treatments seemed to involve needles.

Kirtanananda insisted on going to India with the Swami. There he would take *sannyas* and have the title swami, making him the highest-ranking member of ISKCON. He had his own motives. I never put much value in ecclesiastical hierarchy. "This is not religion; this is knowledge." In the history of our line from five hundred years to the present, the most enlightened devotees were either married householders, *sannyasis,* or Krishna devotees of no particular title. Lord Chaitanya composed the verse "I am not a *brahmin, kshatriya, vaishya,* or *shudra* (the four social orders). Nor am I a *brahmachari, grihastha, vanaprastha,* or *sannyasi* (the four religious orders). I am the servant of the servant of the servant of the lotus feet of the husband of the Braj *gopis* (Krishna), who serve the Lord, the ocean of nectar."

Later I learned that Kirtanananda paid a visit to my mother in New York to let her know I was doing all right in India. He was dressed in a black priest's habit and a black cape. He often tried to present Krishna in many western ways, but Prabhupada's ways were always the most successful.

We arranged visas for Kirtanananda and me, money for tickets, and money to be deposited in Bengal. I was to follow them a few months later.

Swamiji was yelling on the phone to an American banking clerk.

"I want this money transferred to your branch in West Bengal!"

The woman on the phone must have said, "We don't have a branch in West Bengal," because Swamiji hollered into the phone, "Calcutta is in West Bengal! *Chee, chee, chee!*" ("Shame, shame, shame!")

I thought he'd have another heart attack. I said, inappropriately, "Calm down. Calm down!"

Brahmananda, Kirtanananda, and I were in a state of transcendental hysteria, dealing with paperwork, tickets, money transfers, and visas. Swamiji, in charge of everything, was cool as a cucumber.

"Get this bag. Give me that. I will sign. Where's this? Where's that? What is the difficulty? Just put that there."

Brahmananda was sweating all over.

"I got this. I got that. I put that there. No problem."

"Very good. That is nice," Swamiji confirmed.

After a few hours, everything was in place and we settled down.

I had never asked the Swami for predictions or divinations. He had convinced us that spiritual life meant loving Krishna.

Still, I looked at him and asked, "Will I also make it to India and meet you in Vrindavan?"

He looked at me and appeared very young; there wasn't a line in his face.

Then, with a profound expression, he said, "We will meet again in Braj. Rest assured."

Braj, also known as Vrindavan, is Krishna's spiritual abode in the divine sky of Vaikuntha. Lord Brahma, the creator, prays, "I worship that spiritual abode where hundreds of thousands of goddesses of fortune practice their amorous pastimes with Krishna; where every tree is a wish-yielding tree, the water is like nectar, walking is like dancing, speaking is a song, and the flute is a constant companion; where there is the eternal present in time. That realm is known as Gokul (Braj) by only a very few realized souls in this world."

The Vrindavan in India, about ninety miles south of Delhi, is the replica of the original Braj in the spiritual world. Raghunath Das Goswami, a disciple of Chaitanya Mahaprabhu, tells how Krishna told Narada Muni, "Every part of Vrindavan is my abode. The cowherd girls who live here are all advanced yoginis. The forests are like My body, and the Yamuna River is My spine. Demigods from the upper planets live here in invisible bodies. I never leave this land. One who lives and dies here while knowing it to be identical to the spiritual world is never born again in the world of illusion. One who lives here is already living in the divine sky."

The night before Swamiji was to leave for India, I slept in the adjoining room, ready in case he needed more heart massaging, but there was no call. In the morning he lectured as usual. The only difference was today there were three or four pieces of luggage beside the dais, and Kirtanananda was dressed in a suit. As always, even in the coldest winter, Swamiji wore his *dhoti*.

Looking at the portraits of Bhaktisiddhanta and Bhaktivinoda Thakur on the wall, Swamiji said, "I'm leaving you in the care of Bhaktisiddhanta, my guru; and Bhaktivinoda Thakur, his guru—

your spiritual grandparents. The grandparents are always more kind to the grandchildren than the father and mother. So, they will treat you with great kindness. If you chant Hare Krishna, we will always stay packed up together."

He got down from the dais and walked through the hall. We chanted softly as he got into a car with Kirtanananda and Brahmananda.

Before they left, I told them, "I'm going to stay here. I still have to cook. I gotta wash the kitchen floor."

Later, Hayagriva looked into the kitchen and found me on my hands and knees, cleaning.

"What are you doing on the floor?"

"I'm practicing a very advanced *bhakti*-yoga position. You go on now, leave me alone."

three
India

In September 1967, I stood in the JFK Airport terminal with my back to the boarding gate, about to get on an Air India flight to New Delhi. My father, his new wife, my mother, and professor Howard gathered around to see me off. I had a bald head and a *sikha*, and I was wearing a yellow polyester *dhoti* and a white oxford shirt. I carried my beads in the cloth bag and had a small carry-on case. I shook hands with Dad and kissed my mom goodbye.

When I looked back, my dad was smiling with a look in his eye that said, "I wish I was going with you."

First stop, three hours in London. I slept onboard. Next stop, Moscow. Moscow! Why Moscow? Moscow—Russia? Moscow—Krushchev? Yes, and Moscow friend of India. India was involved in many overlapping political arrangements. It was an independent democracy but also a member of the British Commonwealth, along with Pakistan, Ireland, and Australia, even though they didn't share much in common. The principle of Neutrality, included in Indira Gandhi's Fourteen Point Program of social reform, allowed India to accept aid from everywhere.

At the bottom of the steps from the plane stood a Russian soldier in shiny leather jackboots, lots of red ribbons and brass medals, and a welcome-to-Russia smile that scared the hell out of me. He collected our passports.

"You will get them back when you emplane."

It was the first time in over a year that I had to say to myself, "Don't chant Hare Krishna."

The stopover lasted a few hours. I waited in the terminal. I saw hundreds of African students walking to other places in the airport and into buses. When we went back to the steps to "emplane," the smiling Russian guard returned my passport.

On to Delhi:

I arrived in India during the monsoon season. As the plane crossed over the Himalayas that night, constant thunderstorms flashed on both horizons. I thought, *I'm passing through the Causal Ocean, the dark waters that surround every universe, the borderline that separates the planets from the Vaikuntha spiritual sky.*

We landed in Delhi. The plane's doors opened and a wall of heat hit me. I was nineteen, about the same age as the new India.

An Air India minibus took us to a small hotel to stay overnight. I chanted on my beads.

My white bead bag must have looked like a bandage because an Indian woman asked, "Did you hurt your hand?"

"No, these are my *japa* beads."

"I see. Are you here for a spiritual purpose?"

"Yes," I said, "I'm going to Vrindavan."

She pressed a hundred *rupee* note into my hand. In 1967 that would have been about fifteen US dollars, but in India it went as far as a hundred and fifty bucks.

In the morning the bus brought us to the Delhi train station. On the way I saw every manner of transportation imaginable: horse carts, camel carts, buffalo carts, rickshaws, scooters, cars, buses, painted buses, and hundreds of people on bicycles or on foot. Buffaloes and goats were being led about, and cows lolled and ruminated in the middle of the avenues as the vehicles veered around them.

We chugged along on a train that could have come out of the Old West—spewing steam and soot. The monsoon floodwaters had risen up to the tracks and stretched to the east and west horizons. The train seemed to be crossing a clear, calm sea. We plodded on at fifteen miles per hour. It took four hours to go ninety miles.

I was disappointed to see how many Indians smoked cigarettes. Sitting across from me was a teenager who held his cigarette between his first and second fingers, close to the knuckles, and made a loose fist. He drew the smoke through his fist at the thumb, and then flicked the ashes by snapping his fingers. It was a cool move, but his hand must have smelled awful. A cigarette vendor came by, selling cigarettes by the pack or one at a time. The young man bought the last two cigarettes from a pack. Then he began high powered negotiations with the vendor for the empty box so he could boast to his friends like he'd bought a whole pack of butts.

I arrived in Mathura, exhausted and jet-lagged, got off the train, and was surrounded by fifteen rickshaw *wallas* yelling who knows what at me.

One man, in an imitation *sadhu* costume with phony beads and a green turban, shouted two inches from my face, "All temples! All temples! I will take you all temples! We go *now!*"

How was he to know I was not in the mood to go touring "all

temples" after a 24-hour plane trip halfway around the world.

A few days earlier in New York, Hayagriva had told me, "When you get off the train in Mathura, just keep saying 'Gaudiya Math'; you want to go to the Gaudiya Math."

So I kept saying, "Gaudiya Math," the name of the mission of Swamiji's guru.

One rickshaw driver, God bless him, said, "I know Gaudiya Math."

The Mathura Gaudiya Math temple and ashram were on the second floor of a *dharmshala*, a guesthouse for pilgrims. A young swami in his forties, with the same neck beads, shaved head, and saffron dress as Swamiji, met me. He was Bhaktivedanta Narayan Maharaj. Graceful as a cat. Like father like son. His guru's title was Keshari, "the Lion." It was reassuring to see others practicing Krishna consciousness in the same way the Swami had taught us.

"You are a disciple of Swami Maharaj?" he asked.

"Yes, I am Achyutananda."

"Kayachen?"

"What?"

"Have you eaten?"

"No," I said.

Indian culture is most hospitable. "Have you eaten" means "I will feed you; I have food." Not like the Chinese version: "Have you eaten today, or are you starving like me?" He brought me two *kachoris*—salty tarts filled with potato curry fried in *ghee*.

Then he asked me, "You will make *tilak?*"

"Yes."

He gave me a piece of *tilak* clay and a small brass cup of water with a spoon.

"I still need to use a mirror." He handed me a small mirror. I applied the clay to my forehead with my right ring finger, making two vertical lines from my brow to my hairline, and then made the leaf shape on my nose. The two lines represent Radha and Krishna united, and the leaf represents a leaf of the sacred *tulasi* tree. Vrindavan is named after Vrinda Devi, a *gopi* who arranges everything for the rendezvous of Radha and Krishna. She is manifested in this world as the *tulasi* tree.

Narayan Maharaj, the *mahant* (abbot) of the ashram, said, "Swami Maharaj, your guru, is in Vrindavan. Later we will take you there, but now you can meet my Guru Maharaj."

His guru was Bhakti Prajnan Keshava Maharaj, then in the last year of his life.

Keshava Maharaj had been the general manager of Bhaktisiddhanta's mission in the 1920s. He resembled Bhaktisiddhanta in appearance, tall and fair-skinned.

Bhaktisiddhanta's Gaudiya Mission was revolutionary and challenged the authority of the hereditary caste *brahmins*. Bhaktisiddhanta initiated men and women not born into *brahmin* families, and his temple, built at the birthplace of Chaitanya Mahaprabhu in Mayapur, outraged the priests of nearby Navadwip town, on the other side of the Ganges. To collect funds from unknowing pilgrims, they had built a false birthplace in Navadwip, and Bhaktisiddhanta's temple threatened their commercial interests. The caste *brahmins* tried to bribe the Navadwip police to turn a blind eye to their attempt to assassinate Bhaktisiddhanta.

"Sometimes we accept bribes," the police said, "but not for killing *sadhus*."

The police warned Keshava Maharaj of potential danger during the Gaudiya Math's upcoming procession through Navadwip. When the procession, led by Bhaktisiddhanta, passed through the town, people threw stones and bricks from rooftops.

Keshava Maharaj, then a *brahmachari*, and wearing white because of his management position, pulled Bhaktisiddhanta into a doorway and said, "Change clothes with me and give me your saffron robes and *sannyasi* staff. Put on my white clothes and get to the boats to Mayapur. I'll go on in the procession in your place."

That act was considered an omen that Keshava himself would someday take *sannyas.*

Narayan Maharaj took me into the temple; the same room where Prabhupada had been ordained a *sannyasi* in September 1959. Then he brought me into Keshava Maharaj's bedroom. Although Keshava Maharaj was lying very weak and ill, he sat up in bed and kindly spoke to me.

"There are two kinds of sound: material sounds and Vaikuntha sounds. When we make material sounds, we get material things. When we make Vaikuntha sounds, we get Vaikuntha things."

Narayan Maharaj touched my shoulder. We bowed and returned to his chambers. Later, I went off to Vrindavan in a rickshaw with a *brahmachari* of the Math.

The *Adi Varaha Purana* says, "As darkness is vanquished by sunrise, as mountains tremble with fear of thunder, as snakes fear Garuda, the king of eagles, as clouds are dispersed by the wind, as miseries are destroyed by knowledge, and as deer tremble in fear of lions, so are sins destroyed by the sight of Vrindavan."

In Vrindavan, with little effort one can see the spiritual realm beneath a thin coating of *maya,* the illusory energy.

As the rickshaw turned into one of the small roads, I got my first look at Vrindavan. It resembled Hindu Renaissance Europe. Every ornate house could have been a temple; most of them were. Indians are masters of recycling. Stuck on the brick walls of the dwellings were hundreds of rows of cow patties about eight inches in diameter, each with a human handprint in the center. (Could Andy Warhol have done better?) Baked in the sun, they are used as cooking fuel and make a long-lasting hot flame. Yesterday's newspapers were fashioned into paper bags for the markets. Plates and cups were made of either banana leaves or broad leaves stitched together with stems, used once and then thrown into compost pits. Although the style is crude, the supply is unlimited. Clay cups are fired up by the thousands daily and after one use thrown away to melt into the soil.

The rickshaw turned a corner and stopped. Blocking the road was an elephant decorated with heavy brass bells clanging on each flank. He had a huge *tilak* drawn on his forehead.

Now I know I'm in India.

Everywhere people shouted and chanted Hare Krishna.

Just like we do in New York!

Then I remembered that this is where it all started.

We got down from the rickshaw in front of a building near the Radha-Damodar temple. Two gentlemen came out of the house. One man had a swollen cheek. He bent over and spat out a stream of red juice.

I'd better not go to the dentist here.

He was chewing *pan*, a stimulating preparation of betel leaf combined with areca nut or cured tobacco, or both, and spiced with red catechu sauce. Wealthy Indians chew *pan* for its analgesic effect on the stomach after feasting. Poor folks chew it to subdue hunger pangs. *Sadhus* don't usually take it.

We passed through the outer red stone archway of the Radha-Damodar temple, and I saw Swamiji squatting on the narrow veranda. His only garment was made from two yards of cloth tied behind his neck that draped down just above his knees. I had never seen him dressed so austerely. He was cleaning a brass pot, using wet ashes with a wad of straw. Kirtanananda, now dressed as a *sannyasi,* sat on a bench nearby. I bowed down, and they both embraced me.

The building was more than three hundred years old. Behind the outer veranda was the four-foot high door to Swamiji's room. You had to lower your head to get through. His main room was about twelve feet long and eight feet wide, with a stone floor and a window of carved stone lattice. At the other end was another thick, heavy-paneled wooden door. An electric overhead fan moved slowly.

Kirtanananda showed me the rest of the quarters. On the inner porch that overlooked the temple courtyard were two bamboo-framed cots draped in mosquito curtains. At the far end of the porch was a door to the small kitchen, which had a bucket stove (an iron pail covered with clay), and a brass kerosene pump stove. In the corner were a gunny sack of charcoal and some pots and pans. Light came through one window, also carved of stone latticework. *If these walls could talk . . . !*

We walked through the temple courtyard to the side of the temple. Along the path that encircled the temple were two small plaster-covered brick huts. One was the memorial tomb (*samadhi*) of Rupa Goswami, and the other was the memorial shrine of his dwelling. Srila Prabhupada told me how in this courtyard the most confidential associates of Lord Chaitanya, the Six Goswamis, would meet to discuss Krishna concsiousness.

"It is the most sacred and significant place for all followers of Sri Chaitanya," he said.

Rupa Goswami composed his books here—*Bhakti-rasamrita-sindhu* and other writings describing the psychology of the soul and its progress from bondage to transcendental divine love.

When we returned to the rooms, Swamiji was sitting on the floor, having a massage from an Indian man.

"Y'know what's in that massage oil?" Kirtanananda asked with a smirk.

"What?"

"Opium."

I mentioned my arm was sore from the recent small pox vaccination required to enter India.

Swamiji said, "Let this *kaviraj* [Ayurvedic doctor] massage your arm."

A little localized euphoria.

The doctor also taught me to massage Swamiji by starting from the extremities and moving in towards the heart; pushing not pulling.

Swamiji's setup was the same as in New York. He sat on a mat behind the metal trunk that served as his desk. Stacked books lay on either side of his typewriter.

Swamiji dressed me with a one-piece cloth tied behind my neck like his. He showed me how to wear a *kaupin* (Hindu jockstrap) under my *dhoti*.

"If you preach in this dress, everyone will listen. Tomorrow I will give you Brahma Gayatri mantra."

Swamiji followed the system of giving two initiations. At my first initiation, I received the Hare Krishna *maha-mantra*. At my second initiation, I received the Brahma Gayatri mantra and six other mantras. The second initiation seals the relationship of guru/disciple/Chaitanya/Krishna. The Hare Krishna *maha-mantra* is Krishna's 800-number for all to call. The Gayatri mantras received from the lips of the guru are Krishna's private lines.

I slept on the veranda, on one of the cots. In the morning we heard gongs ringing in the Radha-Damodar temple and in surrounding temples. Radha and Krishna arise before dawn, and Their attendants gently wake Them by applying scents, and warm the chilled morning air with *ghee* lamps. If They become too warm, the *pujari* (priest) offers water from a conch shell, and fans them with a peacock fan and a yak-tail whisk. Finally, at the blowing of a conch shell, all are made aware that the Divine Couple are awake.

Swamiji announced, "Later today we have a lunch invitation from my godbrother Yajaka Maharaj."

"But first," I said, "I really have to . . . how do I use the bathroom?"

Swamiji gave me two gauzy red-plaid towels called *gumchas* and said, "Any clothing worn in the privy must be washed. Wear this one going to the privy. After doing your business, wash this in the bucket and leave it to dry. Then you wear this other one back. Never be naked. Take this *lota* [a small pot with a flared rim so fingers don't touch the water] and use this bucket only. Go to the privy behind the *parikrama* path [used by pilgrims to walk reverentially around the temple]. If it is not comfortable, I will get you a commode."

"No!" I said, "I have to learn how to go to the bathroom Indian style."

Besides, I thought on my way to the outhouse, *there are no commodes this side of the Volga.*

I remembered how Swamiji once casually mentioned, "In America you use paper. In India we use water."

And he said to apply the water with the left hand.

The four-foot-square outhouse was behind the walled garden area.

First chakra, *don't fail me now.*

I opened the door.

Now I know I'm in ancient India.

There was no bad smell at all. It had no roof, so the sunshine kept it antiseptically clean. I closed the door behind me and put the bucket and the *lota* on the polished red cement floor. There was a round hole in the floor six inches across. On either side of the hole were two artistically carved male footprints about size ten, width EE. This meant, "Feet go here." I stood in the footprints, squatted down, and, very comfortably, pooped. The scat fell down about four feet—I could tell by the timing—into a large earthenware bowl, literally a crock of . . . (A week later I noticed the crock was empty, recycled by Vrindavan's roaming hogs.) I looked down. The floor around the hole was clean. I had aimed well. Now for the liquid part of the program. Carved into the floor was a dished-out oval area like a small, dry lake, from which ran a curved channel like a dry streambed flowing from the lake. It curved around to the back of the room and was slanted at just the right angle so when urine filled the lake, it would run down the stream and flow out a hole at the rear of the outhouse. What art! So functional! Then I had to clean the Indian way with the *lota*. *I gotta do this!* I poured water on my hand as I reached under. Okay. I stood up and cleaned my hand with slick mud and ashes. No smell. I put the water from the *lota* into the bucket. Still wearing the inside-the-outhouse *gumcha,* I poured the rest of the water in the bucket over my head, hung the wet *gumcha* on the outhouse door, put on the walk-back-to-the-room *gumcha,* took the bucket, and walked back. I thought this whole function was going to be an ordeal and leave me feeling disgusted but on the way back I felt quite civilized.

Wow! I was worried for nothing. I think I'm gonna like it here.

As the story goes, once a *brahmin* evacuated, leaving a very foul smell. He made a disgusted expression.

A voice came out of the stool.

"What are you looking at?" the stool asked. "I was once delicious *gulabjamins* offered to the Lord, and after six hours of association with you, look what you turned me into."

On the walk through the holy village, *sadhus* of all types greeted us with shouts of "Radhe! Radhe!" and "Dandavat, Maharaj. Dandavat."

"Radhe," the most common greeting in Vrindavan, means "O Radha!" and *dandavat* (literally "like a stick") means "I offer my prostrate obeisances to you." Though the title "Maharaj" is meant for *sannyasis,* people in India often use it to address anyone wearing an orange *dhoti.*

We came to a gorgeous garden and temple where an old tamarind tree stood. Yajaka Maharaj greeted us. He looked like my uncle Ernest in saffron robes (but without the cigar). We sat on straw mats, and two *brahmacharis* placed banana leaves and stitched leaf plates in front of each of us. They put a dash of salt in the corner of each plate. Then came the rice. I couldn't believe how aromatic plain boiled rice could smell. Next came the vegetables, with fried curd, cauliflower, and potato. In New York we all had the concept that monks' food had to taste plain.

After a few mouthfuls I blurted out, "This can't be monks' food! This is the most delicious food I ever tasted. The greatest gourmet chefs of Paris couldn't make this."

I remembered that the first verse Swamiji had taught me ("the yoga of kings") ends with the phrase, "This process is joyfully performed."

After lunch, Yajaka Maharaj and his *brahmacharis* started a *kirtan,* and we joined in. He had a golden voice, a full-throated melodic instrument. The *brahmacharis* artistically played *mridanga* drums.

"You see," Swamiji said afterwards, "we do not renounce anything. Renouncing presupposes you own it. But we don't own anything. Krishna owns everything. Just as Krishna steals butter, He steals the hearts of the devotees. He can do this because they're already His. So He is not stealing or cheating; we are stealing or cheating when we enjoy separately from Krishna. We replace the material things with divine things, such as incense to smell. Here is Krishna's beautiful form, decorated with beautiful flowers for our eyes. We have *kirtan* for our ears and *prasadam* for our tongue."

Swamiji then quoted a verse from the *Bhagavad Gita* (2.59).[4] The translation from his *Bhagavad-gita As It Is* reads: "The soul may be restricted from sense enjoyment, though the taste for sense objects remains. But, ceasing such engagements by experiencing a higher taste, he is fixed in consciousness."

"This is the essence of renunciation," he said.

---

4 *visaya vinivartante*
  niraharasya dehinah
  rasa-varjam raso 'py asya
  param drstva nivartate
http://www.asitis.com/2/59.html

A *brahmachari* showed me how to shop at the market. That was sometimes frustrating; every shop had a little sign saying, *Ek dam* ("Fixed price"). However, the law of the land was that everything was negotiable. To buy a half kilo of milk you had to have a two-minute argument; to get *ghee*, four minutes; for cloth, ten; and so on.

Every day, pundits, swamis, holy men, and sometimes college students, came to visit Swamiji. These students were very proud and happy to see Americans in Indian dress, taking up their culture.

"What country you belong?" they asked me.

"I belong to Krishna," I said.

"No, no. He refers to the location of your nativity."

"America."

"Oh! America! What village?"

"What?"

"What village?"

"New York."

They were shocked,

"No!"

"Yes!"

"New York proper?"

It was as if I'd come from heaven.

"Yes! New York, New York. The place is so nice they named it twice."

"Have you seen Banke-bihari?" they asked.

"Who?"

"Banke-bihari, oldest Krishna temple in Vrindavan."

They took me down some paths, and we climbed steps to enter a beautiful marble temple. Inside were at least three or four hundred pilgrims yelling and screaming, "Radhe-Shyam!" and "Banke-bihari *ki jaya!*" (Shyam is a name for Krishna. Banke refers to Krishna's gracefully curved form as He stands with His flute to His lips. Bihari means "enjoyer of delightful pastimes.")

Every day here is a festival. The priests tease the pilgrims by slowly opening the Deity's curtain a few inches to cheers of "Banke-bihari *ki jaya!*" and then quickly close the curtain. Three hundred voices go, "Awww." Then, inch-by-inch, they open the curtain a bit more. "Banke-bihari *ki jaya!*" Then the priests again close the curtain. Then they open the curtain completely, revealing only a straw curtain. "Awww." Then they slowly pull the straw curtain up halfway to reveal only the Deity's feet—and drop it. After ten minutes of this teasing (and when the collection box is full), the curtain rises and stays open all afternoon. Everybody in Vrindavan knows what time the curtain opens, but they still come early.

On the way back I asked the students to teach me a few useful Hindi phrases. I wrote them down in a notebook and practiced them.

I discovered later that in different provinces of India, subtleties of language can make a big difference. For example, in most North Indian dialects, there are two words for hair: *chool* and *kesh*. Sometimes one means hair on the head, and sometimes one or the other means pubic hair. So, if you think you are referring to a woman's long hair, better find out which word to use, especially if her husband is around!

On another day Prabhupada, Kirtanananda, and I got into two rickshaws. We went about four miles through Vrindaban to the Raman Reti area, where Prabhupada's godbrother Bon Maharaj had his ashram. Across the way was a college he had founded with the hopes of it being a spiritual institute, but it became an ordinary secular school.

The gate of Bon Maharaj's ashram was draped in blooming bou-
gainvillea vines. Within was a British garden. On one side was a
small temple of Shiva, his serene face gazing across the path to the
Deities of Radha-Krishna in the temple across the courtyard.

Bon Maharaj came out and greeted us. He was a smooth gentleman with polished European manners. His leather shoes were also
polished. He wore a saffron *dhoti* and a pressed *kurta* (shirt) and had
short combed grey hair. He spoke English with a perfect accent. He
had traveled to the West on the standing order of Bhaktisiddhanta
that all his *sannyasis* must go to the West. Only Srila Prabhupada
had come back with real success. We sat on the veranda, and Bon
Maharaj told us how he met Adolf Hitler.

"I saw Hitler down a long hall. He was pacing furiously. The
war was on. This was before Britain was in the war because the British would never allow any Commonwealth citizen to associate with
the enemy. Anyway, Hitler was pacing furiously down the end of a
hall. He stopped and looked at me. I walked down the hall, and he
immediately shook my hand."

I found this astonishing because it is well known that Hitler
refused to shake the hand of Jesse Owens after the Olympics, yet
he did shake the hand of Bon Maharaj, who was very dark-skinned.

Bon Maharaj went on, "I knew Hitler was trying to find any
kind of evidence to support his Aryan culture. I told him we Indians
are the true Aryan culture from ancient times."

Hitler said, "Thank you," in English and then turned me over
to a secretary/officer who arranged to have me stay with a German
family.

The officer ordered me, 'At the beginning and end of every lecture you must raise your right hand and say, 'Heil Hitler.'

"I agreed. Then he said, 'We really have no need for your lofty ideals.'

"Still, he set me up with a German family in a quarter of Berlin. You should have seen how organized the Germans were. Every day the family would look at a card that would tell them where to stand in the park and at what time the lectures were to be held. Every attendance was marked by a punch mark, like a train ticket. In this way, within fifteen minutes three thousand people assembled. Incredible organizational capacity!"

After *prasadam* in the temple we returned to his veranda. He told us more about Germany.

"I stayed at a German monastery for a few days. They were all so quiet, the black-robed monks, as they walked in groups around the monastery in complete silence.

"The head abbot asked me, 'What do you think of our monastery?'

"I said, 'You won't get mad if I tell you?'

"The abbot said, 'No.'

"'I think it is a house of ghosts. In my ashram somebody's laughing, somebody's crying, somebody's yelling, somebody's shouting, somebody's singing. We feel every emotion at its peak.'

During the rickshaw ride back, Prabhupada said, "He is trying to start a Vaishnava institution to teach spiritual life, but he was persuaded to open up a degree college to get funding from the state government. Now he has to get money from wealthy people, which is then matched by the Uttar Pradesh Province University System. It is not a good business, but I respect his activities and he respects mine."

I typed letters on mailgrams—pre-printed, pre-folded, gummed letter papers that when folded make their own sealed envelopes (a sort of Indian origami).

A lesson on an Indian custom: Don't lick stamps or envelopes, and don't lick your fingers. Actually, don't lick anything unless you can wash your hands before touching anything else. Anything touched by the mouth is considered *muchi* or *jootta,* orally contaminated. Before press-on stamps and envelopes, we had the lick'em kind. That's why post offices all over India have little brass dishes of water to use for sealing stamps and envelopes. The dishes also make excellent maternity wards for mosquito larvae.

The next morning Swamiji announced, "Pack up. We are going to my office in Delhi."

Kirtananda wasn't well, and he had fallen and hurt himself. As a child he'd had polio, which left him with a limp. Now it was worse. He had a bout of dysentery and wanted to go back to America. Prabhupada said that was all right. I saw him off to the airport that week.

We locked up the rooms with locks that looked like they came off Bluebeard's treasure chest. I packed three of Swamiji's metal cases in the back of a horse buggy and helped him and Kirtananda onto the seat. We set off galloping to Mathura train station.

Arriving in Delhi we took a taxi from the station to Swamij's office in Old Delhi. The streets were narrow and winding, and at the end of every cul-de-sac were iron gates the British had installed to control riots.

A beggar came up to the car, thrust his two arms in the window, and yelled, "*Paisa! Paisa!*" (*Paisa* are Indian coins.)

His fists looked like two bloody stumps.

"Oh, Lord!" I gasped.

But they weren't real stumps. He had stuck two pomegranate shells over his hands to make them look bone white with red veins.

I said, "*Chalo jao!*" ("Get out of here!") *Kam karo!* ("Get a job!")

Note to women touring in India: Do not stand in a doorway leaning on one elbow. It's the "I'm for rent" sign.

Swamiji's office was a long room above a Shiva temple. Swamiji gave me a list of things to buy, and I went to the bazaar. Up the street was a row of two-story houses that had six or seven doors. Standing in front of each door were girls about eight to eleven years old. They wore tie-up shorts and no tops and just stood there looking glum.

When I returned, I asked Swamiji, "Who are all these girls? Don't they go to school?"

He said, "They're prostitutes."

"Where do they go?"

"Upstairs."

"Who lives upstairs?"

"Their parents."

Then he said sadly, "This is going on."

He was sitting behind his metal box, writing on a scrap of paper. "Now sit down. I'm composing a verse to describe my preaching mission. *Namas te sarasvate deve.*"

"Doesn't that mean your guru?"

"No. *Saar* means 'son of.' *Nirvisesa-sunyavadi-pascatya-desa-tarine*—teaching Lord Caitanya's message to the voidests and impersonalists in the Western countries."

"Yes, that was me . . . that was all of us."

Later that day Swamiji and I took a rickshaw to a lecture program. At the end of the lane I saw a shop with stacks of folded cloth.

I had only two *dhotis,* one of which was yellow, and the Swami hated it.

"Can I get some *dhotis* from that store?" I asked.

He said gruffly, "Don't talk."

We went on a few yards, and I said, "I do need another *dhoti.* When we come back, can I get something from that shop?"

"Don't talk," he said again.

I didn't talk.

His lecture at the temple was in Hindi, and when we returned in the evening I asked, "What did you lecture on?"

He said, "I blasted them, but they appreciated."

Then I dared ask, "Why was I not supposed to speak about the cloth shop?"

Swamiji said, "It is not a cloth shop. It is a *dhobi,* a laundry. When starting a journey, never talk about a *dhobi.*"

I asked, "But how does that . . . ?"

He cut me off.

"It is superstition."

Then he laughed.

He went on to say more about signs and omens. People observe omens well when their societies have lived together for hundreds of generations, all following the same culture, and have eaten and planted the same foods by the moon and the stars and have shared the same histories.

"In his youth," Swamiji continued, "my Guru Maharaj was also a leading astrologer. He would often consult the Panjika, the almanac."

More signs: Don't begin a journey or an important endeavor if you see or hear someone speak about an oil press, or see empty vessels, a one-eyed man, or a man who has lost his nose. If you leave home and the first thing you see is the back of a woman's head with her hair gathered up in a bun, go back home. Do ask old men for directions. If your urine comes out in two streams, bad sign. Don't ask directions from a cross-eyed man (that was obvious). Do begin an endeavor when seeing a flag, a king, an elephant, a beautiful woman, or a woman carrying full water pots or filling them; when hearing the sound of a bell; or when seeing a calf feeding from the mother cow. Don't travel carrying any kind of oil. When leaving, it's a bad sign if someone calls you from behind. Therefore, if a man is leaving, don't call him from behind; walk up to him and ask him to return. Hearing a donkey bray is bad. Seeing a donkey is bad. Seeing two donkeys is good. Seeing a prostitute, good; two prostitutes walking together, bad. Not because they are prostitutes; it is just a bad sign. If a crying girl passes you on your left side, bad. If a crying boy passes on your right, bad.

Then he said, "*Shuddhu mangsa.*

"What is that?

"Fresh meat."

"Really?"

"To see, not to eat, is a sign of success."

He explained more of the uses of the daily almanac.

"Usually every Thursday afternoon nothing goes well; many bazaars close at this time. But if there is inauspicious sign or time of day and something must be done, we do the needful anyway. But know that it will be done with difficulty."

I spent the next morning looking over *dhotis* in a proper cloth shop and looking out for donkeys, flags, and full vessels. I bought two *dhotis* and hand dyed them with clay saffron color in buck-

ets. There are two kinds of saffron dye. The red clay, called *gherua,*
puts the saffron color on cotton cloth. It also has one other special property: If it is touched by a drop of semen, it makes an in-
delible stain. Even if you wash it out completely white, it leaves a
ring. All sadhus know what that means. *Sadhus* who wear chemi-
cally dyed cloth are somewhat looked down upon. If someone tells
you about a *sadhu* of dubious lineage or character, the first question
is, "Chemical?"

Years later I applied the art of omen-reading with success. A man
said to me, "I'm going to see an important man, but first I have to
drop these clothes off at the *dobhi.*"

I said, "Don't go. Your important man won't be there. You'd
better call first."

He called, and the man's wife answered, "He is not here; he left
this morning for Kanpur."

four
Swamiji Tells Me
Stories to Remember

The Dead Rat Dynasty

WWI, British India, Bombay

A young man stands on the street begging for a few *paisa*. A British police officer in pith helmet and starched collar calls the young man over.

"You look like a bright chap. Why are you begging coins on my block? Don't you know there's a plague goin' on? Look, there's a dead rat. Take that to the police station, and my captain will give you two *rupees*. That'll feed you for a week."

The young man takes the rat in, gets the two *rupees,* and buys a charcoal bucket stove and two packs of *papadums* (thin, crisp crackers). He roasts them and sells them on the street and gets four *rupees*. The next day he buys eight packs of *papadums*. By the end of the month he owns a shop. By the end of the year he owns every shop on the block. He then reorganizes and becomes a cotton broker. Today his family is the biggest cotton family in India. When the men or

women of the family come of age, they are brought into the conference room and are told this story. Then they're given five thousand
rupees each and told, "You have a year to start some business. If
it is interesting, we will support it. But don't ask for more money
because, remember, grandpa started this family with a dead rat."

A person overpowered by the modes of darkness and ignorance
feels uncomfortable in the light and in the company of educated
people. A person overcome by passion becomes restless by the peace
of the mode of goodness. A person in the mode of goodness is always peaceful and comfortable but can become too complacent. The
following story illustrates this.

Once, during a terrible storm, a fisherman asked shelter from a
householder.

The householder said, "You can stay, but you have to leave that
horrible, fishy, smelly net outside."

After nightfall, the householder went to sleep, but he heard the
fisherman pacing in the next room.

"Why can't you sleep?"

"I never feel comfortable without smelling that net."

"Then go sleep on the porch with your net."

Swamiji told me about the Dev family. I had asked him about
Maharajas in India, and he explained that some of them descend
from the sun-god (Surya Vamsa), and some from the moon-god
(Chandra Vamsa).

"But there are others called Maharaja who were made kings
by the British. A servant boy named Deva was engaged in waiting
on dinner tables for the viceroy. Servants are fed first so that while
waiting table they do not look at the guests' dishes with hungry eyes.
After eating, Deva felt tired, and while the guests were in the din-

ing room, he went to the throne room, sat on the throne, and fell asleep.

"During dinner the viceroy kept asking, 'Where's that Davey?'

"After dinner the Viceroy saw his servant asleep on the throne and awakened him.

"'Davey!'

"The servant's first thought must have been, 'I'm finished.'"

Then Swamiji said, "*Sahib shubha*" (association with the British is lucky.)

"The viceroy told the cowering young man, 'So you have some ambition? We shall see.'

"The next day in the *durbar* (royal court), the viceroy awarded a large tract of land to the boy's family and the royal title Dev Maharaj."

Swamiji told me that Alexander the Great was leading a huge army down a road in India. He had chariots and elephants, and they all stopped. Sitting in the middle of the road was an old *sadhu* worshiping the sun.

Alexander got down off his chariot, stood in front of the *sadhu*, and asked, "Sir, is there anything I can do for you?"

The holy man replied, "Yes. Would you get out of my way? I'm worshiping the sun."

Alexander was impressed. The holy man never moved, and out of respect Alexander led his whole army around the *sadhu*.

Swamiji told me the following story about himself.

"When I was a little boy, about eight years old, 1904, the height of the British Raj, my father, Gaur Mohan De, had a cloth warehousing business. He put the business in my name. One day my father received a letter from the stationmaster.

"'Dear Mr. De, you must come to the station in person to pick up your goods and sign for them.'

"He sent me to the station with the house servants.

"The stationmaster called out my name, 'Abhay Charan De.'

"I raised my hand. 'Yes, sir.'

"'You're Mr. De?'

"'Yes, sir.'

"'You? The cloth *walla?*'

"'Yes, sir.'

"'Sign here.'

"The stationmaster sat me on his desk, served me tea, and called in all the staff of the station.

"'Gentlemen, this is Mr. De!'

"They all shook my hand."

On a full-moon night, I went to the roof to see the Jama Masjid mosque, the largest mosque in India. Three huge white domes appeared like full moons growing out of the earth. The Muslims had desecrated many important holy places in Hindu India, including Krishna's birthplace in Mathura, and with the same stones had built mosques on the same sites. They had an "edifice" complex.

Prabhupada was not as much a temple builder as an interpreter of the Vedic literature—a son of the father.

When his spiritual master was having difficulties with his temple managers, Srila Bhaktisiddhanta once said, "Sell the marble in the temple and print books."

Similarly, Prabhupada once asked a disciple, "Where is this money being spent?"

"To build rooms in Mayapur, but we do have to pay some bills from the printer."

Prabhupada said, "No rooms. Books, books, books."

On a new-moon night in Delhi you could see every star and the Milky Way. I saw a blinking star moving slowly across the sky.

An Indian friend said, "That is Russian satellite."

I put down some blankets and sheets and slept in the cool air on the roof. In the morning I awoke surrounded by five monkeys.

Dealings with Monkeys

Monkeys are fearless in trees because they can move in all directions. On the ground or a roof, they're a little nervous. Kind of like us in water—it would be hard to fight in a swimming pool. So, don't be too afraid, but be cautious. They have three-inch canine fangs, upper and lower, and filthy flat nails. They'll do an eye trick with you. They look at you face to face, then look down at your feet and look back up with a surprised expression. So, you look down to see what's wrong with your feet. Then, while you're distracted, they advance on you. When you look back up again, they're baring their fangs two inches from your face, snarling—only to scare, not to bite. Having learned this, the next time I met a monkey who did the eye trick, I didn't look at my feet but stared him down. He walked away defeated. When they come up close yelling and screaming, don't just pretend to go "Boo!" That only makes them crazier. You have to bring it up from your gut, as Bruce Lee says, "with emotional content," and go "Yeaaahhhh!" and they'll walk away and sort of nod to each other like "this guy knows something."

Swamiji's health grew stronger. The *kaviraj* visited him twice a week, always beginning the examination by listening to his pulse. He would hold Swamij's elbow in one hand, his wrist in the other, and move the wrist to his own ear. Three fingers at the elbow were held in three grades of pressure, as were the three fingers at the wrist.

A letter came, and Swamiji announced, "We are invited to Navadwip to attend my godbrother's birthday celebration. We will also see my former family."

five
West Bengal

The twelve-hour train ride was quite comfortable. We brought food, we could rest, and we had good company with other passengers (no smokers). We arrived in the morning at Howrah station in Calcutta and were met by Swamiji's former family, the Malliks. His nephews took us in their car across the Howrah bridge where I saw carriages pulled by scrawny horses.

As I was looking at them one nephew told me, "Don't get close to carriage horses. They bite."

For a bumpy half-hour, we passed through the streets of Calcutta. Many palatial marble mansions from British times were tucked away in the side lanes. We arrived in Swamij's childhood neighborhood. Several four-story apartment buildings surrounded a broad square. The neighborhood looked like a Hindu South Bronx. People were setting up stages and pavilions in the square. The Kali Puja festival would start tomorrow. More on that later.

We walked down a narrow alleyway that opened to a beautiful courtyard where more than fifty of Swamiji's relatives had gathered. His sister, Pishima was a female edition of Swamiji. She was crying

111

"welcome home" tears. She became a grandma to me.

There was a lavish feast and a *kirtan,* and everyone got up and danced with Swamiji.

Afterwards we walked back to the rooms in the courtyard. Now Bollywood cinema music was blasting through the neighborhood. In temporary pavilions furnished with sound systems and raised platforms, the devotees of Mother Goddess had constructed several fifteen-foot-high straw images of Mother Kali and Durga Ma. Bamboo frames are overlaid with straw to fill in the body, which is then covered smoothly with fine clay. When dry, they are painted exquisitely in vivid colors with full attention to detail. Goddess Kali's body is black as night. She wears a garland of freshly cut human heads that drip blood from their throats, covering her upper body. The *tantras* describe that although she is clothed in space/sky (naked), she wears a skirt of severed arms. In one of her four hands she holds a curved sword, in another a lotus, with another she offers the peaceful blessing to dispel fear, and with another she makes the *mudra* (sign) that fulfills wishes.

Mother Goddess's name is pronounced Kaa-li, which is different from the name of the present age, Kali Yuga (pronounced Kuh-li). The zeitgiest Kali is a male deity, made of iron. He brings in the Age of Iron—destruction, ignorance, and confusion. Kali Yuga began the moment Krishna departed from this world five thousand years ago.

On an adjoining stage, devotees built the image of Goddess Durga, who is less fierce in appearance but is the presiding energy of *maha-maya,* "the Grand Illusion." Actually Durga and Kali are different forms of the same personality who serves the Supreme Lord by punishing those who rebel against Him.

Swamiji explained: "Mother Goddess was attacked by a demon, an *asura*, in the form of a buffalo. She rides a lion, or sometimes a tiger, representing her control over the modes of passion and ignorance. First, the tiger attacks the buffalo, the external form of the demon. Then out of the buffalo's open mouth comes the demon in his original humanlike form. Durga kills him with her trident. The buffalo demon represents the living entities, who are constantly changing their bodies, and the trident represents the threefold miseries: *adhyatmika, adhibhautika, adhidaivika*—miseries we suffer, from our present and past actions, in our body and mind, from other living entities, and by acts of nature, such as storms, floods, too much heat, too much cold. This is the conception."

"And Kali?" I asked, a bit afraid of the answer.

"Kali appears that way because the demigods were once harassed by a demon called Raktasura. *Rakta* means blood. Every time you would cut this demon in battle, for every drop of his blood that fell on the ground a thousand more demons would sprout up. Soon the battlefield was swarming with millions of demons.

"The demigods went to Lord Shiva and implored, 'Please save us.'

"Lord Shiva sent his wife Kali, because she is fond of blood. She spread her tongue over the battlefield and sucked up every drop of the demon's blood, and finally the original demon dried up. Drunk with blood, she turned towards the demigods.

"The demigods said, 'Lord Shiva, stop her! Stop her!'

"So Shiva laid down in her path, and when she stepped on him, she stopped.

"'Oh! I have stepped on my husband and have committed an offense!'

"That is the 'photo' that we have. The destructive illusory energy stopped. Durga and Kali can also grant liberation if worshiped very wisely. 'O Goddess, withdraw your illusory energy.' Just as the warden of the prison house has his respectable private life with his wife and family, similarly devotees of Krishna regard Shiva and Devi in their aspects as Vaishnavas. But these people are praying for material benefits—pass BA exam, get good marriage and sons, or cure some illness. The most serious disease is ignorance of our relationship to Krishna."

Beautiful ladies in their finest silks and jewels knelt before the images in tears, sorrowfully beseeching the goddess for boons. Then groups of slightly drunken and maybe hashish-fortified college boys danced a wild Bollywood shuffle on the stage. Then, producing a hidden razorblade, they made two cuts above their left breast, wiped the blood on a betel leaf, and offered it to Mother Goddess. But the most surreal part of the pageant was the music. Blasting on huge amplifiers was India's current number-one hit, not from Bollywood but from Hollywood: *The Sound of Music*. For the pleasure of Goddess Kali, Julie Andrews' soprano voice sang out, "These are a few of my favorite things." Did the devotees of Mother Goddess know what schnitzel and noodles were? A wealthy woman told me she saw the film nine times. Mother Goddess may or may not have been pleased, but John Coltrane would definitely have not approved.

I asked, "Western religions worship one almighty god. These Kali worshipers worship demigods. Who's better?"

Prabhupada said, "Kali worshiper."

"Really? Why?"

"The *shakta-tantras* of the Vedic system will elevate them quickly.

They whisper the mantra into the sacrificial goat's ear that says, 'You will get a human birth and have the right to kill me.' That menans they must understand the science of transmigration of the soul."

A few days later we took a train from Sealdah station, in midtown Calcutta. In 1967 agitations in East Pakistan (now Bangladesh) had begun. Hundreds of refugees lay side by side on the floor and platforms of the station, some asleep, some awake—on guard. I remembered the poem on the Statue of Liberty with the phrase "the huddled masses." Now I was seeing them. They waited for trains to take them to any village in India or to return to their homeland. Or, like the displaced people held over in Casablanca, they could only "wait and wait and wait." Prabhupada looked at me with disappointment in his eyes and gazed with compassion at the crowded, sleeping people.

"If not communism," he said, "what will these people accept?"

While waiting on the platform I saw two signs, one in English and the other in the Bengali script. The English sign said "Commit no nuisance." I assumed the Bengali sign was the translation. After learning Bengali I found out that the lower sign said, *pishabh koribe na:* "Do not urinate." Why was the "do not urinate" sign written in Bengali and "commit no nuisance" in English? Because Indians are masters of political correctness. They have had thousands of years of experience. First of all, Indians consider indoor toilets unsanitary, probably because indoor toilets are. Villagers are not impressed by big-city dwellers' indoor bathrooms. Therefore farmers and laborers relieve themselves anywhere they want, but never in a home. Also, no Indian ladies or gents would go into any toilet with clothes on. Why? No *gumchas* or buckets. Remember what Swamiji said: "Any clothes worn in the toilet must be washed." Second, we know *sahibs* don't urinate on train platforms; they are accustomed to unsanitary yet private indoor toilets. So to avoid offending either group, we'll assume that everyone thinks both signs say the same thing. At least until everybody learns the English and Bengali alphabets.

We boarded the train to Navadwip. The present town of Navadwip is not the same as the Navadwip described in the Vedic scriptures, although it is within the original Navadwip ("Nine Islands"), a sacred land on the Ganges about seventy-five miles north of Calcutta. The *Chandogya Upanishad* describes Navadwip as "a wonderful spiritual city in the shape of an eight-petal lotus. In the heart of that lotus is Mayapur."

Navadwip is the transcendental abode of Lord Chaitanya. This is where my grandsire gurus established their temples. Srila Bhaktivinode Thakur, my spiritual great-grandfather, has described Navadwip, quoting Lord Shiva's discussion with Mother Durga: "O one with the beautiful face, hear in detail how Krishna manifested as the golden avatar now known as Gauranga. O beautiful one, my mouth is burning from the poison I swallowed at the churning of the ocean, and in my mouth I hold the all-auspicious mantra of Gauranga's names. The place of His appearance is a group of nine islands known as Navadwip, and by my order all holy places reside here. Sri Chaitanya appears in Navadwip and distributes the holy name and pure love of Krishna age after age."

Calculated in earth time, we reached Navadwip in three hours.

The deities in Sridhar Maharaj's temple were slightly hidden by narrow doors and curtains. This was designed on purpose, following a custom of Bhaktisiddhanta's that the Deities are not openly revealed. This forces people to strain to see Them and automatically creates a strong desire to see Krishna.

Swamiji and I went up the stairs that led to a wide veranda where Sridhar Maharaj held court. He was older than Swamiji, tall and fair complexioned. Sitting in a Morris chair, he looked like Bertrand Russell in saffron robes. A Morris chair has long, broad movable arms for reclining and supports the legs and back. It is helpful for elderly people with heart conditions and makes a demure throne. Sridhar Maharaj spoke to Swamiji in Bengali and then to me in English with the Oxfordian tones of a highly educated gentleman.

"With very little effort you will be successful in your preaching in India," he said to me.

Swamiji said, "Maharaj is giving you his blessings; just bow down."

I bowed and Swamiji said, "Now go downstairs and see the temple. Talk to the *brahmacharis*. I'm going to talk to Maharaj myself."

After two hours Swamiji came down. We walked to the rooms Sridhar Maharaj provided for us.

On the way I asked, "Swamiji, what were you talking about?"

"If I told you," he said, "you would faint. He is very high."

Vedanta

We returned to the rooms adjoining Sridhar Maharaj's ashram. A tropical sunset only lasts about twenty minutes, and soon it was dark. Swamiji told me to fill the room with frankincense and sit down in front of him. With no emotion he began *Vedanta* talks.

"Sit straight. *Vedanta* means the ultimate conclusion of the *Vedas,* and *sutra* means thread. Very few words to express the widest meaning. Every head of any school of philosophy must write a commentary on the *sutras* to be considered bona fide. These treatises are then verified by comparing them to scriptures, previous saints and sages, examples practiced in their lives, and current living *acharyas. Sadhu-shastra-guru.* This is the system of checks and balances so no nonsense speculative idea can be propounded. There are so many rascals claiming to be this or that god or Krishna Himself. People get cheated by these charlatans who may show some tricks, but they must all pass the *sadhu-shastra-guru* standard.

"In our line a commentary on *Vedanta* is not considered necessary because the *Srimad Bhagavatam* is the natural commentary, describing the qualities of Krishna/Parabrahman. However, in our line from Sri Chaitanya Mahaprahhu to Rupa Goswami comes Vishwanath Chakravarti in the eighteenth century. King Jaya Singh II's pundits challenged that since the Chaitanya *sampradaya* has no *Vedanta-sutra* commentary, it is not bona fide. From ancient times up to less than one hundred years ago, the king's advisors were pundits of the *shastras,* and if anyone could defeat them they could become Prime Ministers, and their versions would become the religion of the kingdom. Vishwanath was in his eighties, so his disciple Baladev Vidyabhushan compiled a commentary on the *Sutras* called *Govinda Bhasya.* When he presented it to the king's assembly, it was accepted.

"The first *sutra* reads *athato brahma jijnasa. Athata* means 'now,' *jijnasa* means to inquire. 'Now we shall inquire into the Absolute Truth, Brahman.' So what does this *now* mean? Now that you have studied the *Vedas;* now that you have performed your duties as a *brahmachari;* now that you are serious in acquiring this knowledge; now that you have understood that impersonal and personal are in harmonious relationship; now that you have understood the eternal constitutional position of the spirit soul; now that you are fortunate to have had a good birth after passing through unlimited lifetimes as human, as animal, as plant, as demigod; now that you have come to this human form of life."

He pointed to me.

"Just like your father gave you the *Gita* when you were young. So you are not an ordinary person."

He closed his eyes and continued.

"Now that you have come into contact with a bona fide spiritual master; now that you are not hankering for material piety, wealth, sense gratification, or birth in the higher planets; now that you have set aside all other inquiries, you can inquire into Brahman."

He paused to say, "Just see how one word—*now*—can have so much meaning."

The world stood still, and so did I.

He continued: "Now we go to the next *sutra: janmadyasya yatah.* *Janma* means creation, source, and cause. *Adi* means—it is the Sanskrit way of saying all the rest, etcetera. And *adi* means the original, the first. Krishna is the cause of all causes and all the rest. So, you can just imagine all the Vaikuntha planets, all the living entities, all the material energies, all the expansions of Vishnu. Pantheism says God does not create the universe—He becomes the universe. And we say that is all right, but it is incomplete, He becomes the universe and remains full in the balance in His own realm. He does not abandon His creations but accompanies them as the Purusha Avatars: Maha-Vishnu, Garbodakashayi Vishnu, and Kshirodakashayi Vishnu, or Paramatma. He is the source of all conscious beings in the spiritual worlds and the material worlds, from Brahma down to the insect. So when the author of the *Vedanta-sutra* says etcetera, *adi*, it is no small thing.

"Then comes *yatah*—"from." God is not a something; He is a

somebody. As Supersoul He is seeing and guiding each living entity's activities in relation with all the other living entities' activities. Every action and its reaction, either suffering or enjoying, is supervised by Paramatma. So how can anyone say, 'I am God?' We all are from something. We can cause energy to change, but we cannot manufacture earth, water, etc. Factories are producing. But they are not producing—they steal what they think is free and change it into automobiles and so on. Transformation of energy is the only thing we do, and then we say, 'Look what I have created.'

"Now the last mantra, and this is very important. *Anavritti shabdat, anavritti shabdat:* "By sound one is delivered." This is repeated; it is said twice. Why is that? Remember what I said: The *sutra* is to use the least amount of words. So why is this repeated? Once would be enough. The significance of repeating this *sutra* is enormous. *Anavritti* means salvation, to be liberated from this material bondage, with no return. *Shabdat* means the sound vibrations of the scriptures, the *Vedas*. The author, Vyasdev, is giving a prophecy of future repetition by repeating this *sutra*. That repetition of sound vibration is the way of deliverance from here to where there is no return. *Harer nama harer nama harer nama eva kevalam/ kalau nastyeva nastyeva nastyeva gatir anyatha*. "*Hare nama*" is repeated three times. That is this Hare Krishna chanting."

We went on chanting on our beads, and that was the end of quite a day.

This discourse also makes the point that Sanskrit, considered the oldest language and full of nuances, subtleties, and scientific use of breath, tongue, lips, etc., could have never evolved from the grunts of primates or cavemen. For example: The Sanskrit name of the demigod of fire is Agni. The Latin word forms of fire—"ignite"—

are not too far off. *Triguna-matra* means "the measurement of three dimensions"; in English, trigonometry. Aside from the similarities in the two languages, this also alludes to the fact that ancient peoples needed a word to measure three dimensions. It also occurs to me that many great sages lived in caves. Hmm.

The next day was the birthday celebration of Sridhar Maharaj. Over six hundred devotees gathered in the temple courtyard, all chanting Hare Krishna and other Bengali songs. On his small throne-like chair, Sridhar Swami was adorned with flowers and garlands. Other holy men in saffron, accompanied by their *brahmacharis* were on the dais. Many present were married householder Vaishnavas with their families.

Swamiji sat in a chair next to Sridhar Maharaj. After several speeches and accolades by the guests, he was showered with more garlands and flowers. But what took me unexpectedly was that I'd never seen a more ashamed expression than his.

Sridhar Maharaj spoke in Bengali, and Prabhupada translated for me.

"Maharaj is saying, 'It is not out of my own personal conceit that I sit here accepting worship like God Himself. I think that even a dog would be embarrassed to receive this kind of grand treatment.'"

There were sighs of respect from the guests.

"'But it is out of duty that I must represent my spiritual master and receive this worship on his behalf. He could not be here today, owing to attending to important business on another planet.'"

There was a grave silence and then more speeches, prayers, and Hare Krishna chanting.

When we returned to Calcutta, Swamiji's relatives provided a nice room in their family temple, Radha-Govinda, in the downtown area. I remember looking out the window and seeing a huge sign that read "Bone-setter." That was a doctor.

Swamiji's relatives and friends and other Calcutta gentlemen would discuss the state of Indian politics long into the night, often punctuated by *chee chee chee* ("shame shame shame").

At one time, after a silence in their discussions, Swamiji said, "Politics means to be polite."

Then after each guest had given his last version of just how things ought to be, they left, one by one.

More Stories to Remember

Swamiji was in the mood to tell me stories.

"All these gentlemen are important. That last man, the fatty one, he was a former minister, and one man before, he is a member of Parliament, but they have no real solution.

"My Guru Maharaj always liked to tell this story:

"'The barge pullers in India walk along the bank of the canals, two by two, side by side.

"'One barge puller says to the other, 'If I ever get rich, I will carpet this path so we never have to hurt our feet on the sharp weeds and rocks on this shore.'

"'So enmeshed is he in his labor that he doesn't consider that when he gets rich he will no longer have to pull the barge. Similarly, impersonal liberation is to become free of the negative experience of having a body. Conditioned by this personal life, and afraid of again taking a form, albeit a spiritual form, they carry over the misconception to the liberated state.'"

I recalled the hobo song, "The Big Rock Candy Mountains":

And the bulldogs all have rubber teeth
And the jails are made of tin
And you can walk right out of them as soon as you are in.
The farmers' trees are full of fruit
And the barns are full of hay
Oh I'm bound to go
Where there ain't no snow
Where the rain don't fall
The winds don't blow
Where they hung the jerk that invented work
In the Big Rock Candy Mountains

"Krishna's divine form is not made of gross matter, only pure spirit. That form is repeated in all the eight million four hundred thousand species of life, but being covered by *maya,* that form is blurred. By deeper observation, the form of Krishna can be seen. The horse walks on its toenails. The foot is there, only covered. The bird's wing and the fish's fin have five "finger" bones.

"But what about trees and plants?" I asked.

"Being overcome by the modes of ignorance, their consciousness and senses are slowed to almost a standstill. Still, Krishna's presence is there. Krishna's quality is that He has interchangeable senses. He can smell or eat with His vision. He can even impregnate the universe just by glancing at it. His vision is three hundred sixty degrees. All His body parts can function like all the others. All living beings possess Krishna's qualities in minute quantity. Trees drink through their legs and eat sunlight with their leaves. The form of

Krishna is there, but is very covered." [Carl Jung would have loved all this.]

Prabhupada wanted me to know about political conditions in modern India. "The new India was considering various political and spiritual solutions to bring the nation into the modern world. Should they align with the West or Russia? Or remain neutral? Would communism work, or socialism, or social democracy? Maybe the British could come back. So many "shoulds," "woulds," and "oughts." Before independence in 1947, British India comprised Afghanistan, Tibet, the entire subcontinent of India, Nepal, and Sri Lanka. After '47 the British partitioned India into East and West Pakistan, Sri Lanka became independent. Under Nehru, we lost Tibet." (East Pakistan is now Bangladesh.)

"Tibet and Sri Lanka separated from what was called a subcontinent, reducing the size of India by over thirty percent. This was the Britishers' parting kick. India is also divided by languages. Most Indians speak three or four: their native tongue, the local provincial language, Hindi, and English."

The Maharajas maintained their power in various ways. For instance, during British times one Maharaja learned to use the system to benefit his own people. The British government paid something to every Maharaj who had aligned with Great Britain. One king demanded an enormous sum of money for his yearly stipend. The viceroy sent an inspector to the king. By protocol, whenever any Britisher came to visit the king, the king had to rise and take so many steps according to the visitor's rank. Some ranks required the king to go all the way to the door to greet the Britisher; some ranks, only one or two steps. This king got up for no Britisher.

The officer, in full uniform, came before the king and said, "The viceroy demands inspection to know why your expenditure is exceeding the stipend."

The king called his *diwan,* prime minister, to show the inspector to the kitchen.

The inspector said to the cook, "Show me how you are spending all this money."

"You see, we use one kilo of *ghee* to cook one *puri;* then we throw the *ghee* out and cook one *puri* in another kilo of *ghee.*"

"Why can't you make more than one *puri?*"

"Maharaj not allow!"

"And just why is that?"

"Some of the good smell of the *ghee* is missing, so we cannot use that *ghee* for the second *puri;* it must be thrown away."

"How many *puris* per day?"

"For Maharaj and family and all, two hundred daily, yes. Now we have the potatoes. Here's three *maunds* of potato [a *maund* is two hundred pounds]. We can only use the five or six potatoes on the top that are not bruised. There cannot be a single bruise."

"What do you do with the rest of the potatoes?"

"We throw out."

"Twenty *maunds* of potatoes for twenty-five people? You must be joking."

"Maharaj not allow any joke. And now here's the *dahl.*"

"All right! All right! That's enough! I can see you're a very dangerous man."

With that, the inspector left. The king was redistributing all the surplus food back to his people, and they flourished, paid for by the British.

One of Swamij's classmates at Scottish Churches College in

Calcutta was Netaji Subas Chandra Bose, later to become General
Subas Chandra Bose.

In Scottish Churches College was a Professor Oaten. In class,
Oaten said, "You natives are not yet ready for home rule. When you
become more civil, then we will grant it."

Later that day, Bose pushed Professor Oaten down a flight of
stairs. Bose was then to be rusticated, meaning he would be expelled
and forbidden to apply to any other college. However, the story
spread to all Indian schools. "Oatenism" became a protest slogan for
Indian independence among college students.

Swamiji said, "In my class one professor was discouraging us
from joining Gandhiji's movement. 'When you are properly civilized we will grant you independence.' All us boys stood up, pointed
fingers at him, and warned, 'Professor, remember Oatenism!'"

Once in British times there was a policeman who stood on a
street in Calcutta and whacked fifty Indians a day with his *lathi*
stick. He would count out loud. He was up to number fifty when
Subas Chandra saw him.

He grabbed the club out of the British officer's hand, smacked
him on the head, and said, "That's fifty-one."

Bose prepared for a military ousting of the British, unlike the
nonviolent efforts of Gandhi. Swamiji told me that history.

"The slogan of the British in India during WWII was, 'We shall
fight the Germans to our last Indian soldier.' Bose made an agree-
ment with Hitler (on the principle 'my enemy's enemy is my friend')
that any Indian soldiers fighting in the British army around the
world, when captured by Germans, would be turned over to him
for his Indian Liberation Army. Indian soldiers started voluntarily
surrendering to German soldiers to join Bose. When England heard

this, they were more apt to give India independence, knowing that their own soldiers were surrendering to the Germans."

I saw a photo of Bose standing on a Japanese mini-submarine.

The British united the territories into one subcontinent under the rule of Queen Victoria in 1857. That was the first time the name "India" was used. Before that there was Mysore, Bengal, Maharashtra, Rajasthan, and so on, from Tibet to Sri Lanka, from Afghanistan to Burma. First England divided and conquered; then they united, centralized, and exploited. In 1947, Indians would decide on forming a government of their own for the first time. That year the British made plans to leave India divided by creating Pakistan (with Mohammed Ali Jinnah as Prime Minister), and India (with Nehru as Prime Minister). They knew Jinnah was ill and did not have long to live. They hastened the partition so fast that the western border of India and Pakistan was drawn in the worst possible way. Or maybe it was done intentionally. Electric powerhouses in Pakistan served towns that were now in India. A railroad junction in India closed because all routes were now in Pakistan. There is even a long length of tracks where the left track is in India and the right track is in Pakistan.

Prabhupada referred to the partition of India as "the Britishers' parting kick." Indian Muslims flowed into Pakistan, and Pakistani Hindus fled to India. The Hindu organization Rastriya Svayam Sevak Samaj (RSSS) rescued thousands of Hindus from Pakistan. Then Pakistan claimed billions in *rupees* for that year's taxes when they were still part of India. Gandhi said, "They are our brothers; we should pay them." This was an outrage to many Indians and the RSSS, and since Gandhi was not an elected official, he was shot.

Swamiji concluded, "As a foreigner wearing *sadhu* dress, you are never to talk politics. I am just telling you all these things for you to know something, but not to talk."

"Some forever, not for better, some have gone and some remain."
—Paul McCartney

It is a great accomplishment that a nationwide civil war in India was avoided. During my time in India, I did feel bad that there were no jokes, no comedy about anything. A joke, after all, is often an insult at somebody else's expense. The only humor acceptable to Indians is puns, as long as nobody gets hurt. Social etiquettes are strongly observed. Most Americans sum up history by three dates: 1492, 1776, and their birthday. Modern Indian history starts five thousand years ago, from the beginning of Kali Yuga. The Vedic culture was replaced by Buddhism; then Shankar Acharya revived Vedic *brahminism*; then the Muslim invasions influenced most of the northern provinces. And most recently India had the Christian British. Vestiges of all these periods in Indian history still exist. That is why many individuals and groups find impersonalism attractive. The Brahmo Samaj and the Ramakrishna Mission in India, like the Unitarians and Baha'i in the West, attempt to unite and thereby sweep away all sects and religions, but end up creating yet another. Swamiji often said, "Everyone's servant is no one's servant."

One of Swamiji's nephews drove us to a festival in a rural village. When we got beyond Calcutta we were soon driving through heavenly groves of banana and mango trees.

"This is the real Bengal" Swamiji said. "I have always wanted to preach in the beautiful Bengali villages."

"Why is that?" I asked.

"Because I've never been there. I'm a Calcutta city man."

When we returned to the rooms there were more than twenty-five letters from America, requesting him to return. The movement had spread to Toronto, San Francisco, Los Angeles, and other cities. Swamiji was feeling in good health.

"I must return," he said. "There is strong movement there."

Then he asked me, "Now, will you promise that you will remain *brahmachari?*"

I said, "Oh, of course! I came to live as a *brahmachari.*"

A few days later he asked again, "After I go back to America, will you remain *brahmachari?*"

I said, "Yes, of course."

Then again, some days later, he said, "So you will stay in my rooms in Radha-Damodar temple. You can go and see the other Vaishnavas there and remain there. And you will remain *brahmachari,* yes?"

"Yes!"

The next day, when I came back from shopping in the bazaar, I saw Swamiji sitting in his usual place with an odd smile on his face. Standing in the room was a woman about nineteen or twenty years old. There was something odd about her. She had a little too much makeup, a little too much cheap jewelry, and was a little too friendly. She stepped up to me, a little too close, bowed down, and kissed my feet—a little too wetly. I stepped back.

"Don't do that!"

Smiling, Swamiji spoke, "This girl is very interested in our movement. Just go and get some more things from the market. She will go with you."

We went out to the bazaars.

She spoke broken English.

"Where are you coming from?"

"New York, America," I said. "I think I'm going to get some sugar-cane juice."

She looked at me and said, "I want your juice!"

"What?"

"Yes!"

"Look lady," I said, "you go that way; I'm going this way!" And I took off.

Up the road was a very important Hanuman temple. At the temple I bowed down to the presiding deity, the huge orange image of Hanuman, the great monkey devotee of Lord Rama. I returned to Swamiji's rooms. I never saw the young woman again, and the question of my remaining *brahmachari* never came up again. A few days later I accompanied Prabhupada to the American consulate. We showed the consul dozens of letters from American students requesting him to return. He was granted a visa. Then we arranged his ticket, money, etc. When he left for America, he gave me the keys to his rooms at the Radha-Damodar temple—and a lot of loneliness.

What can be done with one-on-one association with a great man when the whole world calls? He had to return. What would be my situation? Go and live in the holiest temple in the holiest place of Krishna and have the association of the Vaishnavas who reside there on the banks of the Yamuna. *Mathura Mandala Parikrama*, a sixteenth-century guide to the Vrindavan area (also known as Mathura Mandal), states: "As darkness is vanquished by the rising sun, as mountains tremble in fear of thunder, as snakes fear the lord of eagles, Garuda, as clouds are dispelled by the wind, so are sins destroyed by the sight of Mathura Mandal." In that book, Raghava Pundit, citing the *Gautamiya Tantra,* quotes Krishna telling Narada, "Every animal or demigod who lives in this Vrindavan will attain the eternal Vrindavan in the Vaikuntha sky. The cowherd girls who live here are all yoginis. The five *yojanas* [forty miles] of forests are like My body, and My spinal cord is the Yamuna River, which flows with nectar."

With all that in my favor, I think I'll be all right.

I stayed on in the Calcutta room a few more days. One afternoon two young Bengali men came with a rude demand.

"What is your name, and what is your father's name?"

"Who are you?" I asked.

They didn't answer.

"Where are your papers?"

Had they seen a Nazi movie?

"We are taking you to the police station. We do not know if you are legally in the country. What is your business here? Now come with us!"

We walked a few blocks to the police station and up to the main desk of the day sergeant.

"Officer," they said, "we want to see this man's credentials."

He looked over my papers and saw I had a one-year extension visa. He looked up, his face twisted into a horrible grimace that was almost comical except that he was genuinely angry.

"Now, you get out!"

I froze until I saw he wasn't talking to me but to the two men with me.

"This man is here legally."

Then to me, sternly, "Why are you here!"

I said, "To learn *krishna-bhakti* from the devotees here."

"You mean Hare Krishna, Hare Krishna, Krishna, Krishna, Hare Hare/ Hare Rama, Hare Rama, Rama Rama, Hare Hare?"

He recited the whole mantra!

Then to the two men, "If he wants to, he can stay with me. And you two, I know who you are. Don't ever call the police again for anything; we won't come."

For all travelers in India: As one of Swamiji's nephews told me, "Just know, in every town and village that you go to, within three hours everybody will know you're there.

The story of me, the policeman, and the two communist harassers got around all of India, so I could travel anywhere pretty safely even though many Indians suspected all Americans of being CIA provocateurs. At times I felt I was in danger. Indira Gandhi was blaming every problem in India on CIA provocateurs. One day several members of Parliament came into session wearing buttons reading I AM A CIA AGENT.

six
On My Own: "Temple Boy"

I took the train to Mathura, and then on to Vrindavan by horse cart. I stayed at Radha-Damodar temple, where for several months I studied Bengali from high school textbooks and began compiling Sanskrit and Bengali verses of *Bhagavad Gita, Bhagavatam,* and *Chaitanya Charitamrta.* I would need to know them from memory to use as topics in lectures and to build up an arsenal if I had to debate. Standards are very high in India. A preacher must cite *sadhu-shastra-guru.* As the lawyer in New York said, "Can you imagine a Rabbi who can't read Hebrew?" In the evenings I would visit the temples of Radha-Raman, Banke-Bihari, and Radha-Vallabha.

The pontiff of the Nimbarka sect invited me to sing in the evenings at his temple. Some of his sadhus practiced severe austerities. One of their practices was to wear a finely carved polished wooden belt, as heavy and thick as a banister. It is hinged on one side and on the other side, fitted with a hasp and locked. It hangs loosely around the waist and is worn for four months. This device prohibits the yogi from lying down; deep sleep is impossible. Only an adept yogi can complete this austerity by remaining in trance. It was known that one *sadhu* had done this practice successfully, and many witnesses saw him at two different places simultaneously.

I saw some of their *sadhus* carrying a T-shaped item approximately twenty-five inches long, also made of finely carved polished wood. I asked the leading *mahant* of our sect Vishvambar Goswami about it. "During the *sadhu's* life it serves as an armrest to keep his right hand raised so that his prayer beads don't touch the ground same function as our bead bag. At the time of death it is used as an instrument to hold the yogi's chin tightly shut when sitting in the lotus position. This prevents the soul from exiting through the mouth. *Sadhus* seen carrying this short wooden piece are highly respected."

A warning to travelers in India in the summertime: Do not eat too many mangoes. One mango a day can be too much. They're full of sugar, and sugar is heat. Also, you will see that mango leaves resemble American poison ivy; three leaves, deep green, sprouting together, and red at the base of the stems. You can touch mango leaves, but poison collects under the stem "button" on the mango fruit (a few drops need to be squeezed from this spot before eating). This poison can cause the same kind of rash as poison ivy. I was eating three mangoes a day and within a few weeks I developed a terrible boil, and then dysentery that developed into jaundice.

Dysentery feels like getting punched in the stomach from the inside ten times a day for three weeks. Some friends came to visit me and were shocked at my condition.

"We're taking you to Mathura."

On the horse-cart journey to Mathura I kept hearing the words of Hayagriva back in New York: "Gaudiya Math. Gaudiya Math."

I was fading into delirium. The devotees brought me to the same

Gaudiya Math I'd visited a year before. Narayan Maharaj brought me back to health. I slept for forty-eight hours. I think it was a coma. When I came to, Narayan Maharaj was sitting casually in a chair on the veranda reading a Hindi newspaper. I staggered out on my first day awake. He gestured to me to sit in a chair next to him.

He turned to me and said, "King Luther is dead."

In my daze I tried to unscramble his words.

I asked, "King of Lithuania? Luther who?"

"Your Martin Luther King has been shot. He followed Gandhi, yes?"

I nodded.

He continued, "Yet in this holy place we are very protected from the wild West world."

Later, as I was chanting on my beads on the veranda, I saw standing at the far end of the porch, a very neat looking man in starched white Punjabi pants, a black shawl, and a black aura. He walked up to me and stood silent.

I said, "Hare Krishna."

He said, "*Om.*"

"I'm Achyutananda Das Brahmachari."

He said, "The person standing before you is Yogi Raj Ram Singh."

I looked behind him then realized that this egotist was talking about himself in the third person. Then he appeared to glow in Technicolor, but I snapped out of his spell. Lord Chaitanya describes devotional life as a tender creeper that must be protected by a fence against the intrusion of nonspiritual association. Knowing that pseudo *sadhus* like Yogi Raj abound in India, I built a brick wall around my creeper, cemented with the sound of Swamiji's voice.

The story of an evil yogi and his admiring disciple:

While a yogi was in meditation, his disciple sat near him and prayed, "I wish I could have half of what he is praying for."

Then the yogi heard the disciple crying and came out of his trance.

"Why are you crying?"

"I'm blind in one eye!"

The yogi said, "I was praying for you to go totally blind."

Having recovered from the jaundice, I returned to Vrindavan.

When I got back to the temple rooms in Vrindavan, I went through a bag of English books and magazines Narayan Maharaj had given me. There were English translations of Chaitanya Mahaprabhu's pastimes, some magazines of a Hindu religious society, and a small old paperback copy of *Hamlet*. Sadhus aren't supposed to read mundane literature, but after finishing this slim script of *Hamlet*, I found that Hamlet was a bit of a Vedantist. Actors are often directed to play Hamlet in a way that shows that after seeing his father's ghost he goes crazy, but with the vision of the *Upanishads* and the *Bhagavad Gita*, it can be understood that upon seeing the ghost, he realizes the distinction between the soul and the physical body. It comes up in many places.

Act Two, Scene Two: "What a piece of work is a man, how noble in reason, how infinite in faculties, in form and moving how express and admirable, in action how like an angel, in apprehension how like a god! The beauty of the world, the paragon of animals—and yet, to me, what is this quintessence of dust?"

In *Bhagavad Gita*, Chapter Thirteen, Krishna says, "Knowledge of the field of activities and the knower of activities is described by various sages in the Vedic writings." And in Chapter Seven: "Besides this, O mighty-armed Arjuna, there is another, superior energy of Mine which comprises the living entities who are exploiting the resources of the material world."

Hamlet also shows that he is separate from the body. In Act 5, Scene 1, he comes to the graveyard where, unbeknownst to him, Ophelia is to be buried. He speaks to the gravedigger. This is a meeting of two Danish *sadhus*.

> HAMLET: Whose grave's this, sirrah?
> FIRST CLOWN: Mine, sir. (*Sings:*) O, a pit of clay for to be made. For such a guest is meet.
> HAMLET: I think it be thine, indeed; for thou liest in't.
> FIRST CLOWN: You lie out on't, sir, and therefore it is not yours: for my part, I do not lie in't, and yet it is mine.
> HAMLET: Thou dost lie in't, to be in't and say it is thine: 'tis for the dead, not for the quick; therefore thou liest.
> FIRST CLOWN: 'Tis a quick lie, sir; 'twill away gain, from me to you.
> HAMLET: What man dost thou dig it for?
> FIRST CLOWN: For no man, sir.
> HAMLET: What woman, then?
> FIRST CLOWN: For none, neither.
> HAMLET: Who is to be buried in't?
> FIRST CLOWN: One that was a woman, sir; but, rest her soul, she's dead.
> HAMLET: How absolute the knave is!

Absolute indeed! In the *Gita* (2.19) Krishna says, "He who thinks that the living entity is the slayer or that he is slain does not understand. One who is in knowledge knows that the self slays not nor is slain." And *Gita* 2.22: "As a person puts on new garments, giving up old ones, similarly the soul accepts new material bodies, giving up the old and useless ones."

This is significant for people who practice past-life meditation. They seem to be missing the big question. So maybe you were Cleopatra or Elvis. When you were those people, you thought, "I am Cleopatra" or "I am Elvis." Now you are Leon Pakaknik, or Doris Mandelbaum, or Joe Blo, and you think, "I am this person." The real question is, Who is that "someone" who thinks he is all these persons? You are not Jo Blo now any more than you were Cleopatra or Elvis then—all misidentifications of the soul with the body.

In Act 3, Scene 1, Hamlet contemplates suicide, "To be, or not to be: that is the question: Whether 'tis nobler in the mind to suffer the slings and arrows of outrageous fortune . . ."

Arjuna on the battlefield experiences doubt too: to be victorious in a fight or to live a life of frustrated seclusion. Arjuna says, "Alas, how strange it is that we are preparing to commit greatly sinful acts. Driven by the desire to enjoy royal happiness, we are intent on killing our own kinsmen." (*Gita* 1.44)

Hamlet goes on, "To sleep [die]: perchance to dream: ay, there's the rub."

As the *Gita* says the soul is not extinguished by the death of the body: "The living entity in the material world carries his different conceptions of life from one body to another as the air carries aromas." (*Gita* 15.8) It is also significant that the living entity sees continuation of his personality and doesn't merge into "the big air."

In Act 3, Scene 3, Hamlet, seeing his uncle Claudius at prayer, says:

Now might I do it pat [murder him], now he is praying;
And now I'll do't. And so he goes to heaven;
And so am I revenged. That would be scann'd:
A villain kills my father; and for that,
I, his sole son, do this same villain send
To heaven.
O, this is hire and salary, not revenge.
He took my father grossly, full of bread; . . .
Up, sword; and know thou a more horrid hent:
When he is drunk asleep, or in his rage,
Or in the incestuous pleasure of his bed;
At gaming, swearing, or about some act
That has no relish of salvation in't;
Then trip him, that his heels may kick at heaven,
And that his soul may be as damn'd and black
As hell, whereto it goes.

Or you can go to the *Gita* 8.5: "And whoever, at the end of his life, quits his body remembering Me alone at once attains My nature. Of this there is no doubt." And 8.6: "Whatever state of being one remembers when he quits his body, that state he will attain without fail."

I bought a *dhoti* from a little shop in the bazaar. Vishwambar Goswami, of Radha-Raman temple, came to visit me in the Radha-Damodar temple rooms just when I was unfolding the *dhoti*. The first fold was fine woven cloth, and then as I opened it further, the cloth got thinner and thinner. The last two yards looked like a mosquito net.

Showing the trick cloth I said, "This guy's a shnorer."

"Shnora?" he asked. "What is this, shnora?"

"A crook, a cheat. I'll tell you a story. Once a man died and went halfway to heaven. He met God and the devil.

"They said, 'You are here because you did some good things and some bad things. You can choose between heaven and hell.

"God says, 'Here's heaven,' and shows the man the angels on clouds, playing harps.

"The devil says, 'Here's hell,' and shows him a five-star hotel, a Hawaiian paradise with hula dancers, buffet, water skiing, and entertainment.

"Then God and the devil say, 'Come back tomorrow and we'll hear your choice.'

"The next day he says, 'Well, I think I'd like to go to hell.'

"As the devil brings him down it gets darker and darker and he sees fire and brimstone, monsters, and people boiling in oil.

"'What's this?'" he asks. 'Yesterday, everything was nice.'

"The devil says, 'Yesterday, you were a prospect.'

"That's a shnorer."

Punditji allowed himself to laugh and said, "In our languages that is called a *badmash*, but what does it mean 'hula'?"

"It's a kind of . . . Never mind."

In the evenings all of the hundreds of temples had worship and *kirtans,* and I could attend lectures by Vaishnavas, especially at the Radha-Raman temple. Vishwambar Goswami liked my *kirtan* singing and gave me permission to sing at the Gauranga temple. The pundits at the other temples lectured in Hindi. Many scholars spoke fluent Sanskrit. I didn't. Bon Maharaj spoke fluent English but never lectured in public. I needed to hear from a teacher who could speak

English and answer questions and give explanations like . . . That's when I really missed Swamiji.

One afternoon I went to Bon Maharaj's ashram and met a young American *brahmachari* there. He had been initiated in America by Swamiji as Hrishikeshananda but got drafted into the army and had managed to slip through the cracks of the military system. He told me all about the army, especially the boot-camp training.

"They make you sleep with your gun. My sergeant said I'd never make it, so he drove me in his jeep to the edge of the base and said, 'Go through that gap in the fence and get outa here. Goodbye and good luck.'"

Bon Maharaj was familiar with his situation and gave him shelter in his *math*. In the 1930s Bon Maharaj had converted a German scholar to Vaishnavism, and the scholar had decided to live in India permanently. He had been practicing yoga to obtain mystic powers. The German scholar later noted that all the yogis' mystic powers had been accomplished by modern technology. During WWII, all German citizens living in India were consigned to detention camps (as were Japanese in the US). After much trouble, Bon Maharaj got the German devotee released.

I told Hrishikesh what I'd heard from a Vietnam vet:

"This private comes back to base all messed up—real screwy.

"He says, 'Twenty of us are going down the trail, and we turn a bend. There's this camera set up on a tripod.

'Captain calls halt and tells me this is an obvious boobytrap. What do they think, we're stupid? Boy, are these dinks dumb. Okay, we're all gonna take shelter down in that ditch.'

"Then he tells me, 'Find the longest bamboo pole you can and knock the tripod over. Wait for my signal.'

"I hear Captain's whistle and push the thing over. And then . . . uhhh.'

"The ditch blew up! They're all gone."

Hrishkesh showed me a letter he received from Swamiji. He said I was mentioned in the letter and that it was really for both of us.

The letter to Hrishikesh said, "I suspect that you have interest in taking instruction from some *shiksha* [instructor] guru. I can refer you to one who is most competent of all my godbrothers. This is B. R. Sridhar Maharaj, whom I consider to be even my *shiksha* guru, so what to speak of the benefit you can have from his association. . . . My advice to you both is that you immediately leave. . . . When I was in India, Achyutananda, myself, and others lived with Sridhar Maharaj. He is a very good English scholar. . . . Achyutananda knows him very well. So don't be carried away by whims. Leave Vrindavan. . . . Live peacefully with Sridhar Maharaj, . . . and thereby you will be spiritually enlightened."

Hrishikesh said that Bon Maharaj was teaching him the highest, most esoteric, confidential teachings of *bhava-raga-prema* (divine love). But a few months later I learned he was in Bombay collecting donations for Bon Maharaj's college. I decided to go back to Navadwip.

seven

Back to Bengal

A few days later I locked up the Radha-Damodar rooms, took the horse cart to Mathura and the train to Delhi, and from Delhi took another train to Sealdah station, Calcutta. (I committed no nuisance.) The narrow-gauge line took me to Krishna Nagar, where I crossed the Ganges in a *pangsi* (sampan) to Navadwip. A cycle rickshaw took me through the streets of Navadwip to Sridhar Maharaj's *math.*

I went right up to the veranda where Sridhar Maharaj was sitting in his Morris chair just as I'd seen him months ago. I bowed down, sat at his feet, and told him all about Swamiji's letter to Hrishikesh.

I said, "I just don't know how to relate to senior devotees who have fallen away from Krishna consciousness."

He rose up in his seat, looked down at me, and bellowed, "You cannot say who has fallen from Krishna consciousness!"

After that blast, I put my bones back in their joints and remained silent. Then he sat back, relaxed, and considered the situation.

"Hmmm."

Although his voice was whispery, it combined the tones of Richard Burton, Gregory Peck, a little Charlton Heston, and his own.

Finally he told me, "You must get some better cloth. It is very hot; you will need to wear different cloth in hot weather."

That meant the first lesson was over.

Note: When the temperature is between eighty and ninety-eight-point-six degrees, wear very light cloth; when it's above body temperature, wear heavy cloth. That keeps the heat out.

"We have a small house for you to stay in," Sridhara Maharaj told me.

He took out a thick ragged-edged Bengali magazine (*Panjika,* the daily almanac) from under the pillows of his chair and opened to the middle pages. He looked up at me and said, "Go to the house in the next ten minutes, or wait till half-past three. That will be better."

At 3:35 his *brahmacharis* took me to a little house across the road from the ashram.

Sridhar Maharaj entered later and said, "You will need some sheets. I will provide you with a blanket and a mosquito curtain, and you will need two chairs."

I said, "I don't need two chairs. I can sit on the bed and read or whatever."

Taking the posture of an Oxford dean, he said, "The chairs are not for *you*! If any gentlemen come to visit you, they must be received properly."

I got two chairs. End of Lesson Two.

That night, sleeping was rough. Heat and mosquitoes are normal. What kept me awake were the screams of jackals howling at a full moon.

The next day after morning worship and *kirtan,* one of Sridhar

Maharaj's disciples told me, "Go up. Gurudev is calling."
I sat on the floor of his veranda, he in his chair.
"You are comfortable here?"
"Yes, except for the screaming jackals."
He smiled and went right ahead to his lesson.

"When you were in Vrindavan the main focus was Krishna, but here we are more absorbed in Chaitanya Mahaprabhu. So is your Guru Maharaj. You will have to go to Mayapur and secure copies of the *Chaitanya Charitamrita* and *Chaitanya Bhagavat.* Narottam sings, 'When you dive into the ocean of Gauranga's *prema* [love], you will surface in the ecstasy of Radha-Madhav.' Chaitanya is Radha-Krishna combined—the close embrace of the potency and the owner of the potency."

Although his voice and appearance were very different from Swamiji's, the strength of the meanings in his words felt the same.

"The spirit soul is the ten-thousandth part of the tip of the hair, and just as the sun has sunlight, this spark of consciousness also has an effulgence that is spread all over the body. Whether you are a tree, a human, a demigod, an animal, or an insect, one spirit soul animates your body. An ant is one *jiva atma* [soul], and the sun is one *jiva atma.* So you can imagine how powerful is that one spark of spirit that is in you. You have heard of subatomic particles—electrons and neutrons?"

"Yes," I said.

He continued, "But there are sub-*atmanic* particles: the minute rays of consciousness that spread all over the body from the soul. These tiny sparks of the soul conduct and radiate consciousness to every cell, as when the white blood corpuscles attack an infection. The term *psychosomatic* means mind/body, or better still, self/

body. Mental conditions affect the body. The term is usually used to explain that mental conditions can cause bodily disease. That's all right, but pure mental conditions can cause physical health as well. An example is muscle memory. A maestro pianist will sit before the keyboard, eyes closed, raise his hands, and come down on a perfect chord. The spirit's own body itself is only manifest when we return back to home, back to Godhead, and then generates its spiritual body, which means that in Vaikuntha we are all made of one element: spirit.

"Everything is personal! The only thing that is impersonal is dead matter. Now we are identifying ourselves with the gross and subtle body, and I say it is more like soma-psychotic! They are mentally and spiritually deranged due to the urges of the body and senses dictating orders to the mind and intelligence. All manner of 'isms' are related to bodily happiness. Altruism: The greatest good for the largest number for the longest time. Physical sense gratification for a lifetime of seventy or eighty years apiece—maybe. We bring every living soul to its original state of *sat-chid-ananda*—bliss in full knowledge for eternity. Altruism accomplished!"

Rasology

"From the most dense to subtle, the material elements are earth, water, fire, and air. All occupy the ether—space. Subtler than ether are the mind, intelligence, and ego. The most subtle is the *atma*— soul or life force—which is a separate, nonmaterial element.

"From subtle to gross each property of the subtle exists in the gross. Sound is the property of ether, space. Air includes the properties of space and activates the sense of touch. Then fire possesses space, air, and now light, which gives us vision of forms. Water has all the above plus taste, and earth possesses the properties of all plus smell.

"However, when the soul turns from these gross and subtle elements, he finds his own eternal self. He finds his relation to Krishna eternally in one of the five *rasas*—the finest adjustment of the spirit's love. *Rasa* is the property of the soul in the eternal liberated state. It is a thickening of consciousness."

He hesitated.

"There is no appropriate word for *rasa* in English. The soul expands to an appropriate spiritual form. Krishna's body, abode, and name are all one element: spiritual energy, the finest concentration of spiritual energy. Krishna's name, like Krishna Himself, is not a 'something.' It is a somebody!

"As a seed of sugarcane produces the cane stalk, the seed disappears. The sugarcane juice thickens to molasses; the clear juice disappears. Distilled molasses becomes granulated sugar, then the most dense: rock candy; the *rasa,* or mellow, ecstatically solidifies like a crystal. Each stage exponentially increases in sweetness and possesses all the sweetness of the former. The process from gross to subtle is now reversed! The subtle spirit congeals in *prema!*

"Krishna's body, name, form, and abode are of one element: rarified condensation of spirit. *Sat-chid-ananda* means eternally conscious in divine ecstasy."

He reeled in his chair.

"Krishna doesn't do anything unless it is ecstatic! Sometimes He lets His expansions or demigods accomplish the work. Sometimes He empowers a *jiva* to conduct those affairs, which He enjoys even more. He loves to glorify His devotees. In the *Gita*, Arjuna refuses to fight the battle of Kurukshetra. However, Krishna accomplishes many things in one act. Krishna wants to rid the overburdened world of its evil military might. He wants to liberate the soldiers by having them die in His presence. And He wants Arjuna to accomplish this act. Why does He want this? Krishna tells Arjuna, 'They are already dead; would you like to see? I can finish them all now Myself.' Then Krishna manifests His universal form and Arjuna beholds the warriors rushing to their death into the flaming mouths. But that was not Krishna's plan. Merging into the universe is not liberation. We are already merged in Krishna's universe. It is His pleasure that Arjuna fight as His instrument. That is two of the five moods, friendship mixed with service.

"As you read the pastimes of Krishna in the *Srimad Bhagavatam*, your understanding will be enriched by knowing these ecstatic moods."

I asked, "Do we all have our own one *rasa?*"

"Yes, and that is yours, for eternity!"

"Can you tell me in what my guru's *rasa* is?"

"Yes, I can tell you, but not at this time."

He went on.

"The five *rasas* are eternally within and of the soul, and one doesn't care to change. Once Lakshmi, the goddess of fortune, asked the *gopis* if she could join the *rasa* dance. They replied, 'You must leave your throne and husband, Narayan Vishnu. Then marry a cowherd man here in Braj and be unfaithful to him and join us with Krishna in our secret groves.'

"Lakshmi said, 'I cannot do that,' and returned to Vaikuntha."

"Still, her *bhakti* is enriched by this meeting. Krishna sent His friend and prime minister, Uddhava, to Vrindavan. Uddhava associates with the *gopis* and hears their talks of Krishna in *madhurya* [amorous] *rasa,* but Uddhava never becomes a *gopi.*"

I relished the philosophical principles as much as the ancient histories of the heroes and the eternal pastimes of Krishna with His associates in the groves of Vrindavan. The principles make the pastimes more profound so one cannot mistake them for mythology or ordinary poetry. Not to know the fundamental *tattvas,* or truths, before hearing the pastimes is called *sahajiya*—easy or cheap.

Sridhar Maharaj told me that once Bhaktisiddhanta Maharaj was lecturing at Radha Kund, the pool of Radha and Krishna's intimate love play in Vrindavan. He was lecturing from the *Upanishads.* One by one, the pseudo *sadhus* started to leave.

"He's just a *jnani* [scholar]," they said.

After they all left, Bhaktisiddhanta said, "They are not living in Radha Kund but in *nara kund* [a lake in hell]."

On another occasion Bhaktisiddhanta Maharaj overheard someone in the audience say, "These stories of Krishna in the *Bhagavatam* are for old widows to enjoy."

He once spoke for two months, two hours each night, without going beyond the *Bhagavatam's* second verse.

Sridhar Maharaj continued: "Chaitanya Mahaprabhu came to this world to freely distribute love of God, Krishna consciousness, and to taste and relish *rasas* in the highest and most profound way. He taught all this to Rupa Goswami. The first *rasa* is *shanta:* to be awestruck in Krishna's presence. One is established in Krishna and is no longer attracted by anything mundane. *Stambha*—stunned, paralyzed, is the symptom of this ecstatic identity. In *shanta* your eternal service is as one item of the inanimate yet fully conscious paraphernalia in Vaikuntha. Once there was a king who became Krishna conscious and constantly chanted Hare Krishna. Then he felt the urge of his legs to walk and his hands to do things. He prayed to make them stop, so his arms and legs vanished. Then the hunger of his belly and his sex drive distracted him, so they vanished, and soon he was left with only his head. Krishna embraced the king's head to His chest, and it became the Kaustubha jewel that eternally decorates Vishnu's chest. This is one example of *shanta*. The inanimate objects—the ground, the trees, the ornaments of Vaikuntha—are all conscious devotees. But in Krishna's Vrindavan the trees, the grass, the hills engage in active service."

"How do they do this?" I asked.

"The trees and flowers bloom just as Krishna passes by. The wind, the Dhira Samira breeze, blows through the flowers to carry their fragrance to Krishna.

"This brings us to the thickening of this *rasa* into *dasya*, servanthood: to consider yourself an active servant. Hanuman is the archetype for this *rasa*. Hanuman was sent by Rama to Lanka to deliver the message to Sita that soon He would come to Her rescue. While in Lanka, on his own inspiration, Hanuman set fire to the city. Servanthood is enhanced when the servant goes beyond the call of duty.

"*Sakhya*, friendship with Krishna, includes service and knowledge of Krishna. There are two kinds of the *rasa* of friendship. One kind of *sakhya* devotee prepares dishes for Krishna's meal, waits for the Lord to take the offering, then partakes of the remnants. More intimate are the cowherd friends of Krishna in Vrindavan who do not know or even care that He is the Lord of the universe. They can bite into a mango and say, 'Krishna, I found a good one; try this,' and put it right into His mouth!

"When Krishna accommodates his devotees by becoming their

beloved son, *vatsalya,* or paternal and maternal *rasa,* is the further thickening of *rasa.* It possesses the qualities of the others, and now is added *sneha:* affection, to love Krishna like a mother or father. Knowledge that Krishna is almighty God disappears. Mother Yashoda chases Krishna. 'That brat!—but He is *my* brat.'

"Finally comes *madhurya rasa*! Conjugal love is of two kinds as well: *svakiya,* lawfully married, and *parakiya,* paramour. It is possible to think of a Mrs. God, perhaps, but God's mistress? This is very difficult to understand and cannot be learned until one is eligible. Our Guru Maharaj, Bhaktisiddhanta, was always describing the *madhurya rasa* by explaining what it is not. That is how he taught us to become eligible. That is the nature of *parakiya.* It is not forbidden to know, but it is kept confidential. The Absolute expands His potency, and then He enjoys it accordingly. Krishna is the potent, and we His servants are His potencies. We are the energy; He is the energetic. He is always expanding His energy. Sometimes His energies exceed His own ability to enjoy them. His center is everywhere, and His circumference is nowhere. He is the transcendence that transcends Himself!" (Bertrand Russell would have loved that.)

I ever so carefully put the question again: "You were going to tell me my guru's eternal *rasa?* "

"Yes, I can tell you." Then he paused, "It must be *madhurya,* because of his attachment to *kirtan.* I am also considering him to be a *shakti avesh* avatar [an especially empowered *jiva*]. Sometimes the *gopis* long to be cowherd boys to be with Krishna all day and not have to meet Him in secret. Their prayers were fulfilled when they take birth in Mahaprabhu's pastimes in male forms. But that is enough for today."

He sat back, exhausted. I remembered that he was older than

Swamiji and had weak health. He was on fire! Now his fire was
spent.

"On Earth As It Is in Heaven . . ."

One day a bead on Sridhar Maharaj's *japa mala* broke. It happens
every few years. I helped some of his *brahmacharis* restring them.

You can't just repair one bead; the entire hundred and eight
beads have to be restrung with knots separating each bead from the
ones next to it. First, all hundred and eight have to be strung on
one single thread from a large spool, leaving two-thirds extra to tie
the knots. To get several threads through the beads, you untwist the
thread at one spot and draw the thread through the gap. Got it yet?
I'll put it this way: It is the thread that threads itself! Pulling the
beads draws in two threads, then six threads, nine threads, until they
are tight. Three people are needed to move the beads around so they
don't touch the floor. The *brahmacharis* asked me to help pass the
beads round and round.

The vision: The 108 *japa mala* beads represent the hundred and
eight *gopis*. The head bead represents Krishna. As we chant on our
beads, we remember the pastime when Krishna danced with all His
cowherd girlfriends. Madan (or Kamadev), the lord of lust, wanted
to become famous by shooting his flower-power lusty-love arrows at
sages and saints. One day he approached Narada Muni, the divine
spaceman, and aimed an arrow at him.

Narada said, "No, don't shoot! Making me lusty won't get you
famous. Go to Vrindavan. You'll see Krishna. He is performing His
rasa dance now with His *gopis*. If you can get Him under your spell
with your arrow, you'll be famous all over the universe."

The instruction here is that the devotee does not conquer lust directly, but diverts it to Krishna. Madan hid himself behind some trees in the gardens of Vrindavan and aimed his arrows at Krishna as Krishna and the *gopis* danced round and round. Every time he aimed at Krishna, there was a *gopi* in the way. When he aimed at a *gopi*, Krishna got in the way. This forced Madan to concentrate and meditate on Krishna's divine form. The divine ecstasy overwhelmed him, and he fainted. In this way, Krishna became known as Madan Mohan: "one who can bewilder even the lord of lust."

As we were guiding the beads round and round, I said, "We're helping the *rasa* dance in its form as beads!"

The *brahmacharis* also understood the vision and said solemnly, "*Sadhu! Sadhu!*" ("True, well said.")

A few weeks later all the leading disciples of Bhaktisiddhanta living in Navadwip were invited to present a program of lectures and *kirtan* in a village. I was able to meet the last of the surviving disciples of my spiritual grandfather, my "god-uncles." I went ahead with the *brahmacaris* and Sridhar Maharaj sent us off at the gate and began to dance, *"Hari bol, hari bol!"* For this journey we had to cross two rivers to an interior area beyond the law of any government. They governed themselves. There was the rice family and the banana family, and the Muslims of the community were the wheat and mango family. Hindus and Muslims got along very well, rotating the land in scientific systems as they have done for thousands of years. They were their own law because no government, police, or army could effectively get to so remote a place.

One of the *brahmacharis* brought a slide show. He called it "The Magic Lantern" because it was made out of a kerosene lantern. One night a part in the machine broke.

Our host said, "We will arrange."

From a lump of brass, in a village in the middle of nowhere, someone fabricated the exact sixty-cycle gear to fit into the projector, and *ka-chung*—it worked.

Our host said that the Muslim neighbors wanted to meet Sridhar Maharaj. The next morning we set up a chair for him on the lawn, and about thirty of the elder Muslims came. They were big rough-tough-looking men with beards, yet they shaved their mustaches. Some looked fearful because they used hena, an herb, as hair conditioner. It turns white hair a shocking shade of orange. They all carried long bamboo *lathi* staves and stood silently in front of Sridhar Maharaj's chair, at a respectful distance. We stood by petrified.

After a few moments Sridhar Maharaj raised his right hand, touched his forehead with his fingers, and said, "*Salaam alaikum.*"

They roared back, "*Alaikum salaam!*"

When we arrived back at the Navadwip ashram, the veranda talks continued. Sridhar Maharaj explained that Brahma, the creator, is born in the unformed universe on the lotus that sprouts from the navel of Vishnu. He is surrounded by darkness and creates the sun, moon, and planets.

"Sounds a lot like the book of Genesis in the Bible," I remarked.

"Yes, very good," he said. "Brahma is the highest form of life a soul can attain in this material world. He asked the Lord, 'How am I to create the planets and the different living entities' bodies?' Sri Vishnu answered, 'The patterns and formulae for these creations are engraved on the petals of the lotus upon which you sit.' (DNA?)

"The creator Brahma sees the gross and subtle material elements and weeps. 'Why would spirit souls want to live in this?' And Lord

Vishnu replies, 'It is by their own free desire to enjoy separate from Me.'"

On one stormy night he told me a story about one of our grand-sires, Jagannath Das Babaji.

"In the eighteenth and/or nineteenth century—yes, I said 'and/or,' since it could have been in either century—the one-hundred-thirty-five-year-old Jagannath Das Babaji and a disciple lived in a small hut. One night at one o'clock in the morning, the disciple woke him up.

"'*Babaji! Babaji!*'

"'Yes. What?'

"'There's a feast going on across the river. Can I go? Can I go?'

"'Yes, you can go, but don't eat anything. Thank all the people, wrap up your leaf plate, bring it back here, and we'll look at it in the morning.'

"In the morning they opened up the leaf plate and found a blob of hair soaked in mucus and urine, smelling of sweat, and delicately sprinkled with toenail and fingernail clippings.

"His disciple said, 'What is this? There were hundreds of people there! You told me not to eat. How did you know?'

"'*Brahmachariji!*' Babaji said, 'Nobody gives a feast at one o'clock in the morning.'

"'So, who would do such a thing?'

"Babaji replied, 'They were all ghosts.'"

I walked back to my room in the dark, lightning flashing, and yet had pleasant dreams.

Communism was progressing in West Bengal. There were strikes and bomb threats. The president of Calcutta University was murdered on the day of his retirement. Even in Navadwip homemade bombs could be heard exploding all day, some far off, some near—some too near. There was always a nip of gunpowder in the air. In the rainy season the bombing stopped.

I asked a gentleman, "Has the fighting stopped?"

He laughed, "No, all their powder is wet."

The strikes and demonstrations became so bad that industrialists threatened to leave Calcutta and take their factories back to Rajasthan. That threat slowed down the strikes. A cartoon appeared in the newspaper showing the Chief Minister, Jyoti Basu, scrawling on a wall: DIRTY CAPITALISTS, DON'T GO HOME.

One day I had to mail some letters. I took a shortcut through the forest to the Navadwip post office. A Bengali jungle needs no gardener. Large langur monkeys demurely relaxed up in the canopy of mango and bamboo trees. Serene small black birds clucked musically on the sun-speckled ground. Sweet flowers perfumed the air. This is genuinely a divine place, nondifferent from the spiritual world. The warm breeze touched everything. Was Krishna blowing softly? Off through the jungle was a charming grove. In the golden light I saw four men dressed in black who appeared to be dancing. Yes, they were dancing. They were dancing with sabers. Seeing me, they all stopped. They were the Naxalites, the Communist Party of India Marxist Leninist (CPIML), which was, of course, in all ways and purposes opposed to the non-Maoist CPL Marxists, and both parties were the sworn enemies of the lackey reactionaries, the just plain Communist Party of India (CPI). Street and jungle gangs in India do not name themselves Crips, Bloods, or Satanic Yelpers, but have more politically conscious titles like Liberation Front of Socialist Moralists or The Coalition for Socialist Equality

(Stalinist Maoists) or The Workers Freedom Fighters.

One of the men approached me and asked, "Agent of CIA?"

"No," I said, "agent of Krishna."

"You are the aggressors! You are in Vietnam!"

"No, I am not in Vietnam; I am here in Navadwip."

There was no time to explain that I had no political agenda and that most Americans were against the war.

They rehearsed their rhetoric on me, their first western audience.

"First we took Naxalbari [a village]. Now we shall take all of West Bengal, then conquer India, and when we have freed the laborers from the tyrants, we will drag the capitalist lackeys from their ivory towers and tie them to our yokes and make them plow our fields and we will cut our shoe leather from their backs. Then we shall liberate the whole world. Then, after we have conquered the world, we shall bring nature itself under our control!"

I thought about that a moment and said, "Good plan."

I made my *pranams* and silently remembered a verse describing Navadwip. Lord Shiva says to Parvati, "O girl with the beautiful face, in Navadwip neither an untimely death, a painful death, a violent death, or a peaceful death at home is at all inauspicious. Furthermore, all the results of dying in a yoga trance or in any other holy place are at once attained by dying in Navadwip."

So, I thought, *if they chop off my head or let me go, either way I'll still be in good transcendental shape.*

We parted. I walked on to the post office.

The postmaster was sitting on the veranda, upset because of political agitation.

He looked at me coming and said, "Whatever you are wanting,

I am not having."

"What happened?" I asked.

"Three opposing parties were fighting in the streets, throwing their favorite weapon, the homemade hand bomb—gun-powder, nails, and pebbles wrapped in jute twine. One got through the post office window.

"This agitation was started when some Christians were trying to baptize a Muslim baby and the pastor instructed them, 'You can name your son anything except Allah.'

"The man said, 'All right, I want my son to have a name of God, so make it Jesus.'

"The pastor said, 'In our religion we don't name the boys after Jesus.'

"'All right, but I want him named after God, so let him be called Krishna.'

"The pastor again refused, and the man went and told his Muslim and Hindu neighbors."

Then the postmaster said, "This is all really some political party making trouble. Due to this agitation, I am not opening the post office today, and the magistrate has said okay. This is all due to government, government, government."

"What's today's date?" I asked.

He said, "That I am having: March 23, 1969."

"Y'know what that means? Today's my twenty-first birthday."

"Well, brother, happy birthday."

It was also March 23 in San Fernando Valley, California, at my father's home when a long black Ford pulled up to the front door. The car's tires cut a groove into the lawn, strategically blocking the driveway and front door. Two men in grey suits—six foot two, eyes of blue—rang the bell. My father answered the door.

"Are you Mr. Andrew Barnett, father of Charles."

"Yes, who are you?"

"Selective Service. May we come in?"

"Sure, sit down."

"Do you know where your son is?"

"Yes, he's in India."

"He wouldn't be here, would he?"

"No, he's not."

"Well, if he's in India, there's no way we can protect him."

"Protect him?" my father said. "You would send him to Vietnam or Leavenworth Prison. What kind of protection is that? And, by the way, since you came in here, did you happen to step in something? There's a terrible odor coming from you. Could you please leave?"

"Well, anyway, here's our card."

"That won't be necessary."

My father shut the door.

Sridhar Maharaj's health was failing, and he needed special attention. He sent me to Calcutta to stay with Madhav Maharaj, who had a vibrant preaching program. Sridhar Maharaj gave me a letter of introduction and a fond farewell, then rose from his chair, gave me a blessing with his hand, and collapsed back to rest.

"And from time to time come to visit us," he said.

eight
Kali Ghat

Madhav Maharaj was huge, very fair-skinned, and had small light-brown eyes that twinkled effulgently and never blinked!

"Do you have your passport?" he asked me in a rather high but strict voice.

"Yes."

He looked over the passport and my Indian paperwork.

He must have read my height and weight because he said, "So, I am longer than you. Do you sing?"

"A little."

"Do you know Bengali?"

"A little."

"Do you take rice or *roti?*"

That meant I was accepted.

"Um, both."

"Okay, I like you."

My godbrothers sent me boxes of our magazine, *Back to Godhead.* The cover had a sprawling photo of the chariot festival—thousands of Americans dancing and chanting in the streets of San

Francisco. In the center, standing in one of the chariots, was Swamiji, arms held high, dancing. I showed the magazine to Madhav Maharaj.

Seeing the cover, he yelled, "Go, Swamiji! Go! Go! Go!"

His temple was about five blocks from Kali Ghat (from where Kolkata [Calcutta] gets its name). The great temple and center of Tantric Yoga of the Mother Goddess stands by the Ganges.

Pundit Dr. S. K., in his fifties at the time, and a leading *tantra-shakta* scholar and yogi, and author of several books on political science, astrology, and *tantra,* related to me the following account over several weeks:

"In another age, Vishnu struck Mother Kali with His *chakra* (disc), and she broke into fifty-two pieces. These pieces fell to earth and are now fifty-two holy sites of Mother Goddess Kali. Calcutta means Kali's Ghat. A *ghat* is where steps lead down to a river or pond. The little finger of her left hand fell here. Therefore, this temple is here, and so is the finger.

"Every year on a dark-moon night a certain number of *brahmins*, nine or twelve, come together and worship this finger. Each of them has a key to the locks. (Was Dr. S. K. one of them?) They are blindfolded, because anyone who sees this finger will go mad or blind or even die. They open the lockbox, and inside is another lockbox with the finger. They worship the finger with milk, water, and goat's blood and then return it to its place, locking the boxes with each of their keys. Kali Devi's finger is very soft, just like that of a young girl."

He explained more of the various methods of this system. On a certain holiday, which was coming soon, in the morning thousands of unmarried girls bathe in the Ganges, fully dressed in *saris*. Still wet from the Ganges, they walk up the steps to the temple and pray for good husbands, to heal some disease, or to pass their B.A. exams. Teenage Bengali girls' role models are not Bollywood stars but goddesses and heroines of the ancient scriptures—all denizens of the heavenly and supra-mundane realms: Lakshmi, Sita, Rukmini, Parvati, Gauri. Those girls in their youth, and wearing heavenly silks, even look like goddesses. The gods and goddesses of the *Ramayan* and *Mahabharat* inspire both the young and old. Even the most popular Bollywood star at that time was known for his role as Krishna. Clark Gable, James Baldwin, John Wayne, Gregory Peck, and Brad Pitt have nothing on Lord Ram, Sri Krishna, or Arjuna and his brothers.

Dr. S. K. mentioned that the *shakta-kundalini* yoga method leads to impersonal liberation, but must also be enhanced by the worship of Mother Goddess in all her forms. The process of pleasing the goddess is difficult and very risky, like defending yourself from lower court to high court without a lawyer.

He told me many more aspects of the *shakta* path. Perhaps he was trying to convert me. Ever since Vivekananda, and now Prabhupada and the Maharishi, had American disciples, every guru had to get a white one. I was a prestige symbol.

On Kali Puja night, some *brahmacharis* and I got curious and decided to go see the *puja*. Although we weren't *shaktas*, our curiosity was unbearable.

We took our *harakans* (kerosene lanterns), chanted Hare Krishna with trepidation, and walked across the tram tracks to the Kali temple. As we approached the outer courtyard, we stopped to discuss the daring decision whether to go further, when we noticed that our wooden clogs were sloshing in sticky mud. We lowered our lanterns and looked down. The whole area was wet with goat's blood. Hundreds of goats were being brought to sacrifice.

"We'd better go back."

"Jesus came to save my sins, I hope he kept them 'cause I need 'em again."—from "Rock Island Line," Robert Johnson version

From time immemorial in India, and from the time of Cain and Abel to the time of Christ, animal sacrifice was the method to purchase forgiveness for sins—for the individual, the king, or for the good of the nation. And the coin of the realm was blood.

King Solomon built a temple of the finest marble to be the awe and splendor of the world. Honor was denied his father, King David, because David spilled blood abundantly in wars. King Solomon's temple was the permanent version of Moses's movable tabernacle. Either in the movable tabernacle or in King Solomon's temple, we can envision that from the gate to the altar, the steps were soaked in blood. The front part of the sacrificed animal goes to the priest and the rear shanks to the supplicant.

In the Biblical conception, the animal metaphor of a servant of God is the sheep, which therefore needs the shepherd. The Hindu's mascot is the cow, which needs protection, and the devotee is the protector. Krishna is Gopal, a cowherd boy, and so are His associates, parents, and friends. Does a good shepherd lay down his life for his sheep? Well, let's see—he domesticates them, fleeces them, and slaughters or sacrifices them. The Hindu maintains the cow throughout its life. The cow provides milk and butter necessary for nonviolent human life. The milk, yogurt, and butter are offered to Krishna, and His devotees enjoy the remnants. Humankind can have the animal products without killing the cow. That's the difference between sheepherding and cow protection, and that's the difference between two religions.

In both the Vedic and Biblical systems of sacrifice, sins are forgiven. But most of the supplicants go on sinning again. Prabhupada called this the elephant's bath: "The elephant bathes all day in the river and comes ashore and rolls in the dust."

Just after being released from Babylon by King Cyrus, the Jewish tribes rebuilt the temple in Jerusalem. The Aaronic priesthood was reestablished, and the practice of sacrifice resumed—until Jesus came to offer his body as the sacrificial lamb and to pay the ransom for sin with "his precious blood." He taught the disciples to eat his body and blood, raising bread and wine. Today wholesale animal slaughter is legal but ceremonial sacrifice is banned. Hmmm.

"I woke up one morning and found myself famous."—Lord Byron

A *brahmachari* came to my room and said, "There is one man here with a car come to take you to someplace. He is looking important."

Thank God for a car.

Once, while I was standing in a packed Calcutta bus, a woman asked me, "Could you please move over a little?"

I said, "Lady, my feet aren't even touching the floor."

My chauffeur was Mr. Anil Ghosh, an assistant prosecutor for West Bengal. Dressed in pure white homespun *dhoti* and *kurta,* he was important.

"Everybody is wanting to see the American Vaishnava."

We became good friends. He became my road manager, taking me to villages and suburbs in and around Calcutta to preach and sing the songs of the Vaishnava *acharyas*. Many villages had phenomenal musicians, singers, and drummers. Some of the men, women, boys, and girls had golden voices. Who needs television? Swamiji's mission was flourishing around the world.

I was invited to attend a program hosted by an affluent woman at her British-era marble mansion. The main attraction was a "great mystic" of the Kali persuasion, Sri Mahashay. I was escorted to one of the bedrooms to meet Mahashay. A few ladies and gentlemen of the elite of Calcutta were casually conversing around the king-size bed. Sitting up in bed was Mahashay, smoking a cigarette. He was a tall man in his fifties, dressed in white glossy silks, built like John Wayne, as tan and handsome as George Hamilton. His slick hair was dyed jet-black and combed in a pompadour. His lips were wet and red from chewing *pan*. A black cane with a silver pommel leaned against the bed. He had a black aura. I started to hum the song "Duke of Earl" but stifled myself.

He welcomed me with a regal flourish, then locked me in a fixed stare and started to glow in Technicolor.

"*Tik ache* [That's all right]," I said.

That let him know I had seen that stunt before.

Everyone was waiting to see what the American *sadhu* and Mahashay would do. I was a prop in his show.

He picked up a pack of cigarettes in one hand and a zippo lighter in the other and said, "Radha-Krishna." Then he put one over the other and said, "Chaitanya."

I quoted a Bengali line from the *Chaitanya Charitamrita: rasaraj mahabav dui eka rup:* "Lord Chaitanya is Krishna, tasting the love of Radharani in one form."

"Oh, this is a great man," he said.

He quickly reached behind his back and produced a ripe apple.

So, he's got some cheap mystic power.

I said, "I can buy an apple for fifty *paisa* in the bazaar. Why don't you make a few bushels and we can feed the poor?"

He giggled nervously.

He must have been out of tricks because he signaled that we all go into the living room. It was furnished with modern couches, devans, and armchairs and filled with incense and cigarette smoke.

Without warning, he nodded to the hostess and said, "It's time!"

He escorted one of the gentlemen into a side room. I sat chanting my beads. The other guests sat in silence, waiting for something to happen. After a few minutes we heard a hideous death shriek, followed by bitter weeping from inside the room.

The guests smiled to each other and said, "The *darshan* (vision)!"

The door opened. Mahashay came out of the smoke-filled room looking a little pale. Behind him was the gentleman, his eyes swollen and red, sweating and recovering from something horrible. He collapsed in a chair.

Terrified and still weeping, he managed to say, "I saw her . . . Ma! . . . Kali Ma!"

Could Aleister Crowley have done better?

The next day I met Dr. S. K. on the steps of Kali Ghat.

"I know this Mahashay. He is a cheap cheat. He has the long tongue."

I said, "He didn't speak much."

"Not like that," the doctor corrected me. "Not *a* long tongue; he has *the* long tongue. I will explain after some time. It is just like some circus trick. He is mentally deranged in a religious atmosphere." He sighed. "This is going on."

I was invited to the cremation ceremony of a very important holy man, the founder of a Shaivite mission who played an important role in India's Independence Movement. Over five hundred people attended. Many of them were members of Gandhi's Congress party and were living national treasures of India. I even recognized members of the Communist Party of India, who showed no shame in attending this most religious function. Dr. S. K. was there as well.

In the courtyard behind the ashram, His Holiness's body lay on a bed of flowers over a mound of sandalwood. *Brahmin* priests chanted Vedic mantras. When they finished the invocation prayers, the women—wives and daughters of the dignitaries—intoned the soprano vibrato *ulu-ulu,* which sounded like a chorus of goddesses in mourning. All could feel they had bid the soul farewell.

Then three torch-bearing swamis, who were well-known in the freedom struggle, lit the wood. As the flames rose, the smell was like—the only word I can use is barbecue. (Now, now, vegans and vegetarians don't turn up your noses. These bodies we inhabit are not dust in the wind but meat on the bone. It is a rude awakening. Forgive the rudeness; appreciate the awakening.) All present were enlightened in knowledge of the soul as separate from the body. There was no weeping or sadness.

Then came an even ruder awakening. The skull was punctured with a sharpened bamboo spear. It is customary that the youngest disciple perform this duty. The brain tissue spilled out into the fire, sizzling in steam and smoke. Yet no one showed a trace of horror or disgust. All watched, perfectly aware that this was the body and not the person.

His successor swami then embraced me and gravely chanted, *"Shiva Shiva Hara Hara Shambu Mahadeva Deva Hare Rama Hare Krishna."*

nine

Tantra

(Bet you turned to this chapter first, huh?)

Overview

Mantra, *yantra,* and *tantra* are three dimensions in yoga systems. The main connotation of the term *tantra* is strict and flawless execution of rules and regulations. *Tra* means to deliver, to liberate. *Yan* refers to mechanical designs. *Yantras* are geometrical diagrams and formulae drawn on paper or engraved on copper plates and used for concentration or as blueprints in the construction of buildings. Temples in India are constructed according to *yantras* that correspond to the deities to be worshiped in them. Moses' tabernacle in the wilderness, Noah's ark, King Solomon's permanent tabernacle in stone and cedar, Stonehenge, the pyramids of Egypt and Mexico—all are full-scale architectural versions of *yantras* (for those with an edifice complex).

Man means the mind. Mantras—Vedic hymns, the original sound vibration, *shabda brahma, nad brahma, om,* and the Hare

Krishna *maha-mantra*—are chanted to deliver the mind. Chaitanya
Mahaprabhu taught that the Hare Krishna *maha-mantra* "cleanses
the mirror of the mind."

Tan means the physical body. *Tantras* are practices to deliver persons strongly attracted to the bodily conception of life. *Tantras* liberate by the practice of anatomical endeavors involving the microcosm
of the body.

Tantra is misunderstood as indulging the senses to a level of
exhaustion to reach superconsciousness. (More accurately, most ill-
informed practitioners would probably get sick, drug-addicted, or
die.) It is also wrong to think that *tantra* is for sex, e.g., "I practice
tantra yoga" (wink, wink). The *Kama Sutra* is not *tantra*.

"As I always say, it is better to look good than to feel good."
                                    —Fernando Lamas, on his wardrobe

Hatha-yoga, taught in many fine studios by very competent instruc-
tors all over the world, gives practitioners excellent physical health,
but many *hatha*-yoga schools ignore the health of the spirit soul
and teach impersonal meditations. Krishna says in the *Gita* (12.5),
"For those whose minds are attached to the unmanifested, impersonal feature of the Supreme, advancement is very troublesome. To
make progress in that discipline is always difficult for those who are
embodied." He describes the body as the external dress of the soul.
Keeping the dress in good condition and neglecting the wearer is
ignorance. Still, once on a morning walk on Juhu Beach, Bombay,
Prabhupada saw a man standing on his head. A disciple walking
with Prabhupada was insisting that he is not "one of us" and not
"our man."

Prabhupada paused awhile and then said, "This is very healthy. All you do is eat."

The Ascending Process: Shakta Kundalini Yoga
("I remember when you were just a glint in your daddy's eye.")

INTRODUCTION

To introduce this matter it is necessary to understand the position of Lord Vishnu, Lord Shiva, Goddess Durga (the material energy), and we, the finite living beings.

Krishna, the Supreme Personality of Godhead, is the only enjoyer. His varieties of energies—spiritual and mundane, subtle and gross—are all meant for His pleasure. The living beings are of two types: eternally liberated souls who exist in loving service, and the souls eternally in material bondage. We are in bondage because we want to be the enjoyer. ("Better to reign in hell than serve in heaven.") Being tiny particles of spirit, we can be overwhelmed by the material illusory energy, enjoying and suffering. How Krishna accommodates the souls in matter is explained as follows:

A portion of Krishna known as Maha-Vishnu expands His material nature to fulfill the desires of the souls who wish to enjoy matter. He infuses material nature with these souls by casting His glance at the deluding energy known as Durga. Krishna never touches His material energy, but Durga is not entirely cut off. This glancing at the material goddess issues from between Maha-Vishnu's brows, and a halo is created (as a corona appears during a solar eclipse). This halo is divine Shambu (Shiva), the masculine symbol, emblem of Vishnu. This halo is the dim twilight reflection of the *brahma-jyoti*, the effulgence, and the goal of impersonalists. This masculine symbol functions as the male seed-giving father of the mundane world in the form of the glance of Maha-Vishnu.

Shiva is compared to yogurt, which is milk tainted by acids. Sada Shiva comes into contact with the stupefying illusory potency Maya and the multitude of living entities frantically desiring to enjoy. For anyone unfamiliar with the subtleties of Vedic cosmology, a Tom Waites song is a loose translation: "There ain't no devil. It's just God when He's drunk."

The intercourse of these two (Shiva and Maya) brings living souls from Shiva into the womb of Devi. It is the male infusing the life-forces into the material womb. Although cosmic in scope, it is actually mundane sex. (The Big Bang.)

This Vedic description of how souls are put into the material creation has some parallels in the Old and New Testaments. "That old serpent called the devil and Satan, which deceiveth the whole world, he was cast into the earth and his angels were cast out with him" (Revelations 12:9). To further the parallel, Lucifer means light and Shiva is compared to a halo. Both are "cast into the material world," infusing matter with the living entities. They both provide the living beings with what they desire: the illusion of ownership and enjoyment.

But now the parallels part. Shiva presides over the dark mode of ignorance, but he is not ignorant, nor is he rebellious towards God like Satan, an Anti-God. The individual spirit souls are envious of God. Prabhupada's example: "The warden of a prison is a government official. Although both he and the prisoners live in the prison, the warden is not a prisoner. He can execute or release prisoners according to the laws of the state. Similarly Shiva and Durga can put the soul in bondage or grant liberation. The prison warden also has his private personal life outside the prison where he and his family mingle with law-abiding citizens, governors, and even the President."

This is Sada Shiva and Parvati of the Vaishnavas. The Biblical version makes no distinction between the custodian and those in custody. The Durga *maha-mantra* describes Durga thus: *deva devotami devata sarva bhauma ananta koti akhila brahmanda nayiki:* "You are the Supreme Goddess of all other gods and goddesses throughout the unlimited millions of universes." (Sorry Mr. Hawking, but "multiverses" have been known in the Vedic culture since, literally, the dawn of time.)

PART ONE

In the tantric scriptures, Shiva describes the hierarchy of his energies (*shaktis*) in all their female forms, Kali being the most destructive, along with her six expansions: Dakini, Rakini, Lakini, Kakini, Sakini, and Hakini. In some places she is said to have nine forms. One of them, named Cinnamastha, I saw worshiped at the Kali Puja celebrations in Calcutta. Her sky-clad (naked) body is blood red. She stands on the forms of Rati (desire) and Kama (lust), who are engaged in sex. In one of her four hands she holds a curved sword. She severs her own head, and two fountains of blood spurt from her headless neck. In one hand she holds her own head and drinks her own blood; in another she holds the head of a demon who drinks from the other fountain. By this image she certainly teaches the benefits of celibacy. These features of Mother Goddess are worshiped in their forms from hideous to heavenly with all their paraphernalia in Shakta temples throughout West Bengal and certain parts of West India. These agents are also present in the six *chakras* and influence the entire material nature. Parvati is Shiva's consort in the highest capacity. Shiva is also known as Shankara, Rudra, Pashupati, Hara, Shambu, Mahadev, and many other names. His consorts are known by the names Durga, Bhadrakali, Chandi, Ambika, and others.

Flawless practice and strict adherence to rules and regulations require the yogi to remain silent for days or months at a time. If a word is accidentally spoken, the vow is broken, and he must start over from day one or wait until the next year when the planets and seasons are in the proper position. Or the guru can advise alternatives to counteract the breach of practice, such as sitting in the "five fires": The repentant yogi sits in the center of four fires, one in each cardinal direction, and the overhead sun is the fifth. The neophyte tantric yogi goes through a period of austere apprenticeship and Vedic purification rituals at the Kali, Durga, and Shiva temple functions and makes pilgrimages to holy places sacred to the Goddess. He memorizes and studies hundreds of Sanskrit verses. Strict *brahmacharya* (celibacy), is practiced, their clothes dyed with *gherua* (clay, no chemical). During this time the *ashtanga* (eight-limbed) yoga system's *pranayama* (breath control), is practiced. This saturates the body with pure oxygen and clears all seventy-two thousand *nadis* (bodily channels; literally "rivers").

The Shakta yogi goes to a cremation ground and searches through the ashes to find the one part of the human body that does not burn. This cylindrical piece of tissue, about two inches long and a half-inch thick, is situated behind the navel and smolders with an eerie green light. The yogi must say the appropriate mantras and, without disdain, eat it. This *tantra* propitiates the goddess of the third *chakra: manipuraka,* at the navel. He must drink wine without being influenced. This pleases the fourth goddess, residing in the *vishuddha chakra,* at the throat. All this prepares the yogi's nerves and emotions to be completely indifferent to the urges of the body. Shiva is named Pashupati, the lord of animals, and is worshiped with the next *tantra.* The yogi sits in a circle of five different animal heads arranged around his mat. A priest invokes the animals' spirits, and they attack the yogi's mind. If the yogi goes mad, that's the end of the road for him. If the yogi remains sane, he can go on to the next stage: Kundalini sex yoga.

PART TWO

"As above, so below. As without, so within.
As to the left, so to the right."

Perfecting the sequence of *nauli* exercises trains the yogi's rectal abdominal muscles to function in reverse. This creates a vacuum by which the yogi obtains the fuel to propel his life airs up the *sushumna,* or central, main river. (Another name for a yogi is *urdhva reta:* "one whose semen rises.") Only when this stage of yoga is perfected may he obtain the "fuel" from a female yogi, or yogini. Yoginis usually have the title Bhairavi, wife of Shiva, and nobody offends, abuses, or messes with the Bhairavis. I saw one Bhairavi who was in her seventies. You could tell she must have been very beautiful as a young woman, but now her face was wrinkled and her hair pure white. I got a short glimpse of her wearing only her *gumcha* when she finished bathing. Her body was as young and smooth as a fourteen-year-old girl's. The Bhairavi assists the yogi by producing and delivering the necessary fluids, using breathing techniques very similar to Lamaze exercises. During intercourse, the yogi must control his mind and constrict his stomach muscles so that he does not only not lose any seminal fluid, but also draws the yogini's fluids into his body.

As described in the introduction, in the process of the primordial creation of the cosmos, Lord Shiva, the symbol of masculine mundane procreation, infuses the female Mother Goddess Durga with the individual living souls, thereby entangling them in matter. Tantric sex is the reenactment of this cosmic event on a human scale—in reverse! When the yogi and the Bhairavi engage in sex, they identify themselves as Shiva and Durga by the *mantra shivo 'ham* ["I am Shiva," or "I am Shiva's"]. The yogi, in the role of Shiva, symbolically liberates the living entities entrapped by Maya by withdrawing them back into himself. Durga, played by the Bhairavi, graciously releases the souls from her illusory power.

The *ida* and *pingala* are two of the major rivers, or channels, of energy that begin their upward course from the base of the spine, rising left and right. They crisscross each other, and a *chakra* is situated wherever they intersect with the central river, the *sushumna*. This is seen externally on a grand scale where the three sacred rivers of India—Ganges, Yamuna, and Sarasvati—meet at the *triveni* ("three rivers") at Prayag (Allahabad), at Navadwip, and at the Bay of Bengal. The ocean's infinite waves represent the thousand-petal lotus.

On the cosmic scale, this is duplicated in six of the planetary systems of each universe, Brahmaloka, the highest abode of the creator, being the seventh lotus of a thousand petals, the *sahasrara*.

When the presiding Dakini of a *chakra* is pleased, and they are very easily displeased, they grant permission for the yogi's subtle body to enter their realms. The Dakinis are just as bound by the laws of *tantra* as is the yogi. While he is in the abode of any one of the six goddesses, which may be for only a fraction of a second, the yogi's training in temple worship and study of the scriptures comes to his aid. He then worships her with the mantras and parapher-nalia learned in the neophyte stage. Imperfectly performed worship, now or in the past, offends the goddess, and she deploys her powers of illusion, reveals one of her horrible forms, and casts him out. He will remain outcast and be afflicted with madness, incurable disease, or death. Or, if less offended, she may offer the yogi one or all of the eight mystical perfections.[5] If he accepts them, that's the end of another road. If she is pleased by his worship, she is obligated by the mandates of *tantra* to withdraw and allow him to ascend to her sister goddesses above. These *tantras* must be done according to each of the six goddesses' standards of worship. For example, if the yogi is in the presence of Sakini and attempts to propitiate her with mantras or paraphernalia dedicated to Hakini, both goddesses will be angered, and then . . .

PART THREE

If the yogi remains determined in his goal to achieve liberation, the goddesses—under obligation to Mother Durga, the tantric regu-lations, and now the yogi himself—are duty bound to assist him.

---

5 The mystic powers are (1) to become lighter than air (levitation), (2) to become heavy and immovable, (3) to become large, (4) to become small, (5) to reach great distances to obtain anything (a la Sai Baba), (6) to create your own planet, (7) to have multiple forms (sorry, 12 max per yogi), and (8) to subjugate others.

We are unimpressed by the yogis or Mahashays when they display mystic powers because they are all failed yogis. Had they been successful, they wouldn't be here.

They withdraw their powers of illusion, both horrible and sublime, allowing the life-force to rise up the *sushumna,* carrying the yogi on his path. When the yogi is ready to attempt liberation, he prepares the "long tongue" by cutting the tissue that connects the tongue to the lower palate (*frenulum linguae*) so he can extend his tongue below his chin and up to his eyebrows. Then *pranayama* breath exercises saturate the blood with pure oxygen to provide the yogi with up to two to three minutes of external consciousness and seven to ten minutes more of internal consciousness. He can continue only in a controlled dream state. (This talent is acquired during the five-animals ceremony.) Then he takes his last breath and, sitting with one heel blocking the anus and the other pressing down on the femoral artery, inserts the long tongue into the postnasal passage, blocking the throat, mouth, and Eustachian tubes. Now all the nine gates of the body are sealed. Then he amalgamates the five vital airs, including the airs that lie dormant in the body (the gasses that cause a dead corpse to float). All are fused into one condensed gaseous fuel. When the time of liberation is decided, and all the gatekeeper goddesses have withdrawn, then can the yogi ignite the vital airs with the flame of *kundalini* and propel his soul upwards through the conduit of the *sushumna* with the force of a pneumatic power tool. This fractures the fontanel (*brahma randram*), and the soul can enter the Brahman effulgence.

But wait! Not so fast! Madhwa Acharya explains, "Standing on either side of the fontanel are two Vishnuduttas, guardian-messengers of Vishnu. Each holds a trident and will stop any ineligible yogi from achieving liberation, in case any of the Dakinis were too merciful." But, as often happens, the fallen yogi will probably make the mistake of thinking he has become God, because one glimpse of liberation, although momentary, is more ecstatic than any mundane pleasure. Prabhupada calls this "the last snare of *maya*."

Prabhupada gave the example of an astronaut in outer space who's always looking down to the earth planet. He is connected with cables to the ship and is always talking to earth on the radio.

Kundalini yoga is a Hindu Tower of Babel, or like digging a tunnel to escape a prison. If the prisoner is caught escaping or later caught out in the free world, the punishment is the most severe: solitary confinement.

ten
Prabhupada's Return, 1970

I received letters from Brahmananda every week telling of Prabhupada's travels throughout the world, and I learned he was returning to India to organize the construction of an international temple in Mayapur.

Prabhupada sent Jayapataka Brahmachari from America to join me and help arrange for his arrival. Jayapataka looked like a college football quarterback. He stayed with me at Madhav Maharaj's temple. We transferred money to different accounts in Indian banks to buy land in Mayapur.

Jayapataka was expert in everything, but he kept eating with his left hand. The *sadhus* would not allow that. You're not even to touch your plate with your left hand.

"No! No! No! You must not do that!" they scolded.

One old sadhu made Jayapataka drop rice from his left hand.

When I saw him repeat the transgression, I said, "Jayapataka, sit on your left hand!"

He shifted to one side and sat on his hand.

"Okay, now eat," I said.

The *sannyasis* all looked on in approval and said, "*Sadhu! Sadhu!*"

We traveled to Mayapur to look for land and stayed in an ashram belonging to Prabhupada's godbrother Bhakti Saranga Goswami, who had passed away some years before. In each corner of our room were large piles of black unhusked rice.

"Okay, Jayapataka," I said, "they are storing rice husks for three or four days in these dark rooms. Scorpions are gonna be hatching out of these piles of rice, and that's why we have to sleep in here."

"Why in here?"

"Because they're going to hatch, then crawl under the doors and out onto the veranda, then out into the fields to live their lives in peace and not get squished by us. We're going to sleep in the middle of the room so they don't crawl over us. That's why we're not on the veranda getting in their way."

"I don't think you should scare me like this."

"I'm not saying this to scare you. It's harvest time. Get into a position so comfortable that even in sleep you won't move."

Nobody moved that night except the scorpions. Neither Jayapataka nor I did any flapping.

In the morning I opened the door and felt something very light hit my head. I brushed it off, and what looked like a tiny black lobster was a baby scorpion. He wasn't cute.

Prabhupada was set to arrive in three weeks. We arranged a twenty-car motorcade to escort him from the airport to a two-story residence we'd rented in Calcutta. We alerted the newspapers.

At the airport I ran to where Prabhupada stood, bowed down, and kissed his feet. Five or six of the generals of ISKCON accompanied him. He had given some of them the order of *sannyas*. He had big plans for India; he wasn't just passing through.

"It's hip to be square."—Huey Lewis

Shortly after Prabhupada arrived in Calcutta I approached him with a request.

"Now that the preaching is going to be widespread in India, I would like to preach as a *sannyasi*."

"Yes," he replied, "and Jayapataka too."

Some days later we collected the paraphernalia for the fire sacrifice, prepared our *tridandis* (the triple staff of a mendicant), and took *sannyas*, receiving the "Swami." To live up to the *sannyas* standard and receive honor is a serious responsibility. *Sannyas* is an established religious order, not hippie counterculture. In India, *sannyas* is part of the establishment, and the establishment is hip.

The *sannyas tridanda* represents the three-part principle of dedicating mind, body, and words to Krishna. By his clothes and *tridanda*, a *sannyasi* is declaring publicly that he is dedicating himself to Krishna, and he's asking people to govern him accordingly and keep him in line with his vows. For example, I was walking in Mayapur with another swami when we encountered three Vaishnavi widows who bowed down to us on our right side.

I asked my companion, "Why did they do that?"

"They do not want to step on our shadows."

I thought, *I may have the title "His Holiness," but I'll never be that holy.*

Prabhupada told me all about his travels throughout Europe, Asia, America, Canada, Japan, and Africa. We went to Delhi to hold his first *pandal* program. A *pandal* is a temporary pavilion similar to the movable tabernacle of Moses, but ours was equipped with stage lights, microphones, speakers, seats, and carpets. The *pandal* was large enough to accommodate the five thousand people who attended the programs each evening. We even had a huge kitchen put at the back to provide *prasadam* for all five thousand. *Atithi devo bhava*—even an unexpected guest should be treated like a god. A similar line is in the Bible: "One should greet an unknown guest, for in doing so he may be entertaining angels."

One of the benefits of taking *sannyas* was that I didn't have to wear, or wash, the five-yard *brahmachari dhoti*. Swamis wear a cloth half as long. When the program was over, white cloth on the *pandal* posts was left behind, so I cut some up and dyed (with *gherua*) enough clothes to last a year.

At the Delhi *pandal* Prabhupada instructed me to go to Mayapur and build a cottage on the land we'd bought, to accommodate him and several disciples. He gave me all the dimensions, even down to the ratio of sand to cement (4/1) for the brick foundation. The upper structure was to be of bamboo and thatched grass on a three-foot plinth. It was to have an outdoor privy.

When Prabhupada visited there sometime after its completion, he said, "A cool cottage. It shall be named Achyutananda Cottage."

Krishna Fulfills All Desires

When construction of the Mayapur temple was soon to begin, for three weeks a relentless caravan of bullock carts loaded with bricks, cement, sand, gravel, and steel rods slowly rolled onto the property. Workmen unloaded materials at strategic parts of the acreage to be used in the various sections of the guesthouse and temple. For security, we hired ten soldiers of the famous Gurkha Regiment of Nepal. (The term *gurkha* is derived from *go-rakha,* "protector of the cow.")

One day a young Communist walked up to the cottage. I

could tell he was a Communist because they were boycotting Indian clothes (in open defiance of Gandhi's homespun-cloth movement). They wore plain Western clothes, and his were the plainest clothes I'd seen yet. I was sitting on the veranda of the cottage.

"Why are you hiring foreigners?" he asked. "They can steal and go back to their own country. I am Bose. I will supervise the security with my men."

"What do you know about security?" I asked.

"I have studied all the military strategy."

"Okay," I said, and called over one of the Gurkhas.

Their legendary weapon, the *kukri,* an eighteen inch curved chopper, was on his belt.

I said to the Marxist/Leninist, "You two fight, and whoever wins gets the job."

As tears filled his eyes I noticed his left hand quiver.

"Wh . . . what do you expect me to do?"

I replied, "I expect you to die, Mr. Bose."

He walked off with a whimper. (I had been waiting for the chance to say that to someone who deserved it, ever since Goldfinger said it to James Bond.)

Later that year Prabhupada visited Mayapur with several disciples. As we were walking around the paddy fields one day, we came upon one of the irrigation gullies crisscrossing the fields. I always took a running leap to cross these, but Prabhupada leapt across in one step. I turned to Bhavananda, and we just looked at each other with our mouths open. We'll never know how he did it.

Bhavananda told me an amazing story.

"Prabhupada and I are leaving a department store in New York. We come to the revolving doors when a customer holding shopping bags gets in first. Prabhupada gets in the next section and moves ahead as the door turns, but the man stops to fumble with his bags, stopping the doors and trapping Prabhupada inside. I run out the side door to get the man to move on, but when I get outside, Prabhupada is standing on the street, looking around for me."

"So?"

"So the man with the bags is still in the revolving door!"

"Then how did Prabhupada get ahead of him?"

"I don't know!"

The Songs

The first stage in a *sannyasi's* life is called *kutichuk,* when he resides in a cottage outside his village and usually composes a commentary on a book to eventually be the foundation for his missionary life. I composed the book *Songs of the Vaishnava Acaryas* at this time.

The songs I learned are known all over Bengal and Vrindavan wherever our sect established worship in temples, monasteries, and homes. Great devotional singers like Krishna Das Babaji and Yajavar Maharaj, and countless *sadhus* and householders I met taught me the words and melodies, and the *mridanga* drum. A *mridanga* is made of fired clay. It has one small side and one large bass end and produces dozens of sounds. There are hundreds of songs written by Rupa Goswami, Bhaktivinode Thakur, Narottam Das Thakur, and others, and they all have a message, a teaching. The songs are expansions of the Hare Krishna *maha-mantra.* They describe the stages of devotion in solace, enthusiasm, longing, hoping, celebrating events, and remembering Krishna's qualities and pastimes. For example, during the *brahma-muhurta,* an hour before sunrise, Radha and Krishna are awakened with a slow song in the Bhairavi Raga, a scale in which every interval is minor. In this way They are awakened, not with an alarm, but with a melody as gentle as a lullaby. All the songs have exquisite themes and melodies. I am sure that Brahms, Ravel, and Rachmaninoff would have borrowed from them, and of course Richard Strauss would have definitely stolen them.

eleven
South India

The second stage of *sannyas* is called *bahuduk*, which means to live in many different residences, not being attached to any one home. As someone said, "*Brahmachari* and *sannyasi* means those who can hang all their belongings on one hook." I wrapped up three sets of *sannyas* dress and tied them with the *kaupin* underwear. I also had a brass *lota,* some books, and shaving gear, and I included my first aid kit. My specialty, learned from my own experience, and some barbers, was the treatment of infections. In the tropics, infections spread quickly and must be treated in a certain sequence. Don't touch, don't pick, don't scratch. In my kit was a bottle of pure chlorine, tubes of antiseptic cream, a variety of needles and tweezers, cotton swabs, gauze, adhesive bandages, glycerin, and Epsom salts. I was the boil doctor.

The *brahmacharis* designed the perfect minibus for our trip. Then, with another *sannyasi* and half a dozen *brahmacharis,* I headed off to tour all the major holy places in South India.

"All temples! We go all temples! We go *now!*"

191

The *brahmacharis* arranged programs and places for us to stay, sometimes in bare public guesthouses, sometimes spoil-ya-rotten, lavish marble homes. We were invited to attend a great gathering in Sri Rangam, one of the oldest and largest Vishnu temples in India. The *mahant* showed us a series of twelve oil paintings of the twelve major temple festivals.

"Marshall Tito of Yugoslavia came to visit in the 1950s," he said. "We did not allow him in the sanctum sanctorum, but he could attend the festivals outside. He commissioned these paintings."

How remarkable, I thought.

Another temple, in Udupi, was established by Madhwacharya eight hundred years ago. (Hare Krishnas have a disciplic relationship directly to him and his successors.) Madhwa's followers are known for their strict execution of ritual worship of Krishna. The current pontiffs welcomed us lavishly.

One of the *acharyas* asked me, "Why is your doctrine called *achintya-bhed-abhed?*"

I answered, "Krishna is simultaneous one with and different from . . ."

"Yes," he gently interrupted, "I understand different and non-different. But why *achintya,* inconcievable?"

I said, "Mundane scholarship, yoga, and austerities cannot help one attain Krishna."

I quoted the *Brahma Samhita:* "When the eyes are smeared with the ointment of love of Krishna—*prema anjana*—then Krishna reveals Himself in the hearts of saintly souls. He possesses inconceivable qualities."

His grave silence indicated he liked this version. His response was better than any applause I ever had playing music.

We were not invited to the Uttaradi Math, also established by Sri Madhwa. It is further inland from Udupi and over the centuries became extremely insular and sectarian. They only initiate those from their own brahmin families born in their provinces. Their slogan is that there are only two kinds of living entities: brahmins born in our families, and everyone else—and everyone else is a *rakshasa* (a hideous atheistic monster).

I thought, *Let's go anyway. If they don't even allow brahmins from outside their provinces, wait'll they get a load of us untouchables from across the black ocean.*

We started to go, but the bus's gas tank was leaking. One of my *brahmacharis*, a good auto mechanic, looked under the bus.

"Can you fix it?" I asked.

"Not out here. I need bubble gum."

"Come on, there's no bubble gum this side of the Volga, you must know something else."

"I know bubble gum!"

We didn't go.

Prabhupada once told me one of his godbrothers, a brahmin by birth, visited him in our Vrindavan temple. After conversing for hours about the success of the Hare Krishna movement, Prabhupada invited him to take *prasadam*. His goodbrother's pleasant mood changed.

"If it has been cooked and touched by the foreigners," he said, "I would prefer not to, thank you."

About a year later Prabhupada told me, "He has just now sent me a letter saying that he received a donation of an old temple, and asked if I could give him some funds for repairs. I have responded that the money has been handled by my foreign disciples, so it is tainted and you would not like to touch it."

I have heard that this swami kept that letter with him his whole life. He left this world at age 104.

In the morning my host, a wealthy industrialist, drove us around the Udupi temple grounds. When we arrived at the main entrance, the temple manager stopped us. He was angry, saying we should not have been driving on the road. He began shouting at me.

We all argued awhile until my Indian host told the manager, "You cannot talk to Swamiji like that. You are just a salaried man."

At that, the temple manager cringed in shame. Embarrassed, he meekly withdrew and walked back into his office. Why? The term *salaried man* had called up the caste card. In the caste system even a one-acre potato farmer can command more respect than a salaried president of a corporation—because, be he ever so humble, the farmer has no boss.

Sometimes *a shudra* (labor caste) may be rich and influential. For example, during the time of Lord Chaitanya, Ramananda Roy was of the *shudra* class but was the prime minister to the king.

The names Das, Gupta, and Sen are titles of the Kayastha *shudra* caste in Bengal. Gupta means secret, Sen means military, and Das means servant. Das Gupta is therefore a secretary, or can even imply a Secretary of State. Sen Gupta means military secretary or even Secretary General. The *Gita* says that the castes are divided by the nature of one's work and character. They are not inherited.

In one of the courtyards of the eighteen-hundred-year-old temple was a marble hall whose floors and dome provided perfect acoustics with just the right touch of reverb. Sitting at the end of the room was a maestro playing a *shenai* (a double-reed instrument akin to the European concert oboe or English horn but with the volume and range of a soprano saxophone). He played so legato that the horn made streaming sheets of sound, moving from mixolydian mode (the Blues), to dorian minor, to Lydian natural minor, to harmonic minor. (Thank you, Mr. Greenburg.)

"Do you hear that?" I asked one of the *brahmacharis*, a former saxophone jazzman.

"I sure do. He sounds like John Coltrane bouncing riffs off the universe."

"If he breaks into 'My Favorite Things,' I'm going to faint."

John Coltrane would have approved.

A Bollywood movie came out that lumped the Hare Krishna devotees in with hippies. People were constantly harassing us with a dumb song from the film *Dum Maro Dum,* village slang for pot smoking. Our Indian supporters hated it. "Now everybody is singing that stupid song." Many Indians could not distinguish between the different foreign national cultures. (How many westerners can tell the difference between a Bengali, a Punjabi, or a Madrasi?) For instance, one Indian gentleman who used to visit Prabhupada frequently in Calcutta brought up the subject of the caste system.

The man said, "You see, Prabhupada, in India we have four castes: brahmins, *kshatriyas, vaishyas,* and *shudras.*"

My mouth dropped open, and Prabhupada retorted, "Yes, I know that."

Everyone in India knows the four castes. Then it occurred to me—this man thought Prabhupada was an American.

I went to the Bombay home of Devanand, the director of the *Dum Maro Dum* movie. I took along my godbrother, Bhagavat Das, who was Prabhupada's chauffeur and bodyguard. Standing at over six feet tall, he was three feet wide. We took a 16mm projector and a twenty-minute documentary of our international movement showing the temples, book production, dairy farms, and children's school. After some struggle, the director let us in his home and we showed him the movie on his private screen. He apologized.

All devotees of Krishna respect Lord Shiva, but we object to Shankar Acharya's proposal to superficially worship the five deities, a practice called Panchopasana. These five are Vishnu, Shiva, Ganesh, Durga, and Surya (the sun god) and are to be used only as "tools" by less spiritually advanced people for concentration. In the advanced stage, worshipers abandon these gods as no longer necessary because they believe that both the soul and the deity merge into "the big air." ("I now pronounce you null and void.") This means the worship, the worshiper, and the worshipful are temporary and false. ("Till death we are apart.") This is an imitation of devotion. Buddha rejected the Vedic culture. He threw out the baby with the bathwater, and Shankara brought back the bathwater without the baby.

As Vaishnavas we believe that Krishna, His devotees, and our individual relationship to Krishna are all eternal. *Bhakti* is practiced at all levels, by the neophyte and by the fully realized souls who are beyond liberation. *Bhakti* continues in the Vaikuntha sky, unrestricted and everlasting.

We visited a village in Madras sacred to Lord Shiva where nine Shiva *lingams* are worshiped. There are many Shiva *lingams* all over India, and these nine were considered the most ancient. The *lingam* represents male and female on the cosmic scale. (This symbolic image illustrates the point Prabhupada told us about Freud when he said, "Everything movable and immovable in this world is due to male and female combination.") There are very few restrictions for worshiping the *lingam*. All may enter any temple and offer water and flowers. These *lingams* were all made of the same hard light-grey stone, deeply pockmarked by thousands of years of dripping water.

Our host told us how these nine Shiva *lingams* had been established.[6] Many ages ago a king asked the sage Agastya Muni to kill two *rakshasa* (demon) brothers. One demon would kill his brother and cook him in a stew. They took turns doing this. They would invite local *brahmins* to dinner and serve them this dish. After dinner the host brother would call out, "Brother, come out!" and the brother in the stew would tear out of the *brahmin's* stomach and re-amalgamate himself, and the two brothers would feast on the dead *brahmin*.

Agastya Muni went to the *rakshasas* and said, "You may kill me and feast on me."

They killed him, cooked him up in a tasty stew, and ate him. Then Agastya Muni tore out of their stomachs and came back to his natural form. The demons were properly cremated at this place. Agastya Muni established the nine Shiva *lingams* to commemorate this episode.

"If you're so smart, why ain't you poor?"—from *A Thousand Clowns*

Prabhupada admired Gandhi's hope to develop India as a nation of self-sufficient villages, just as Gandhi admired Tolstoy and Thomas Jefferson for their same vision. The Talmud describes a rich man as

---

6 The host's version was based on ancient scripture, and perhaps folklore-embellished over centuries.

one who is satisfied with what he has.

Prabhupada explained: "The more one has a higher spiritual taste, the greater the share of spiritual power and proportionally less dependency on material things. None of the political systems will help mankind if there is only godlessness, and all systems can be successful amongst God conscious peoples."

About five miles outside downtown Bangalore we visited a family that lived on a one-acre compound. The brick and thatched-roof house had five bedrooms and was simple but not austere. Had it been made of marble it couldn't have been more comfortable. They had a paddock for four cows and a calf. Their concrete tanks, filled from their well, provided water year round. In their kitchen and pantry were "hundred pound" of everything. Their only electric appliances were a radio and a fan. In the kitchen and privy were two fifteen-watt light bulbs. On their altar were pictures of Krishna, demigods, and Gandhi, as well as a bag of salt produced by Gandhi in Bombay during his march to the sea. This event is as significant in India as American's Boston Tea Party.

We were invited to see the family's morning *puja*. The Deity was baby Krishna—brass, three inches tall, and holding a sweetball. The mother of the house bathed Gopal in milk and water. Then she lifted him up in her hand and tossed Him into the air. The brass Deity did a somersault, and she caught Him in her hand and said affectionately, "Hey, Gopal!" Then, after applying *tulasi* leaves and sandalwood paste to His feet, she dressed Him in silks and solemnly recited mantras. All over India, women rich and poor worship baby Krishna in motherly affection. There are no strict regulations, and sentiments are freely lavished.

To earn money, the family had joined the community and engaged sharecroppers to grow varieties of grains, fruits, and jute. I was surprised when they told me they only do sharecropping occasionally and haven't needed much money in three years. "It is a botheration." Their lives were enriched by their worship, temple festivals on holidays, and inviting pundits, storytellers, and musicians to lecture and perform. Many groups—from small associations to mighty nations—have tried communal living, but not having a share of spiritual power, they either dissolved or slowly became dependent on technology and financial complexities.

We arranged a large gathering in downtown Bangalore. After one of our lectures and *kirtans,* an uninvited gentleman sat next to me onstage. He had three horizontal lines made of grey ashes across his forehead and a large red *tilak.* This is the emblem of the Shaivites, who are usually impersonalists. He spoke into the microphone and praised us for adopting Hindu culture; then he went into his *shpiel.*

"Devotion to Krishna is a must—until you come to full knowledge and become one with Brahman."

As he got up to leave, I took his hand and said, "Punditji, wait a bit. You know the *Gita,* I'm sure."

"Oh, yes."

"Then you must know the two verses in the ninth chapter that start, *maya tatam idam sarvam:* 'By Me this entire universe is pervaded.'

"Yes," he said, "He is everywhere and all-pervasive like the formless air."

I continued, "But then Krishna says, 'Everything created does not rest in Me': *na cha mat sthani bhutani.* And also in the *Gita* Krishna says, *avyakta vyaktim apanam manyante mam abuddhaya:* 'Those who think form comes from formlessness have no intelligence.'"

He squirmed a bit and said, "Well, *mat sthani* can mean . . ."

I interrupted him, "I know you are a Sanskrit scholar and can quote many *yadvah yadvah* synonyms, but what does it say as it is?"

He went silent.

I saw a few heads nod, and a few gentlemen said, "*Sadhu! Sadhu!*"

"I'm gonna lay my head on that lonesome railroad iron, let that midnight freight train pacify my mind."

—from "Trouble in Mind Blues"

An impersonal idea of Buddhism is that consciousness evaporates into nothingness. This is actually spiritual suicide, to cease to exist. But as warnings on prescription drugs say, "If thoughts of suicide occur, discontinue use."

In Bangalore a journalist featured my lectures each day in the local paper. He told me he was the correspondent for the paper assigned to Cape Canaveral to cover the American space program.

"I met Werner Von Braun, and we discussed transcendence," he said. "He confidentially told me he was building a rocket with recyclable fuel and would send it to the end of the universe to find heaven. I said, 'You're building a rocket like a Tower of Babel.' He got offended and ordered me off the premises."

We traveled to Bhopal, Madhya Pradesh, for a weeklong Hare Krishna festival at the Lakshmi-Narayan temple built by Mr. Birla, a major Indian industrialist. Our guide took us up a hill to show us the view. On the horizon were three tall factories.

He explained: "Our main bossman here is having three sons. This factory on the right is for his first son, second is for his middle son, and that one to the left is for his third son."

Way off to the far left we saw a smaller factory and asked, "What is that factory?"

"Hah! He is having one bastard son, so he set him up with his own factory as well."

Crowds attended every evening, and we were invited to private homes every day. After one lunch, our host bade us farewell, saying, "I think my family has gotten rid of much bad karma by feeding you all here today."

I silently gulped.

One night our projector broke down. Our host borrowed one from the local family-planning department, whose workers said they wanted to operate it for us. I think they just wanted to see our movie.

"How's the family-planning movement going?" I asked.

"Not too well."

"Really, why not?"

"The villagers like to have big families. They are telling, 'One more mouth to feed means two more hands to work.'"

At the end of our stay, the temple managers called us to the office.

"I will tell Mr. Birla of the successful program—ten thousand people per night!"

I had no idea; beyond the stage's footlights I could see only out to the fifth row.

"There is also some donation for you from the collection box, sixteen thousand *rupees*."

I accepted graciously and offered some money to the manager. He graciously refused.

A Halava Story

A year later, a man known as "the *halava* king" donated land in downtown Hyderabad for our temple. *Halava* is a sweet made all over India. But the *halava* king's secret recipe is similar in taste and texture to gummy bears, only cut in cubes and sprinkled with powdered sugar. They are now famous all over India. The "king" had been offered large sums of money for the recipe, but never gave in. When he was young and poor he sold his *halava* on the streets on a small folding table. Standing next to the table were his only two milk buffaloes. Thinking that it would be good advertising to decorate them, he went to the *chor* bazaar, the thieves' market. There you can buy anything, no questions asked. He saw two long, thick, brass chains that would look pretty on his buffaloes and bought them for a few *rupees*. When he got home he realized how heavy they felt. They were pure gold. The merchant thief didn't know. That's how the *halava* king started his fortune.

The First Mayapur Festival

The first international gathering of Hare Krishna devotees was soon to be held in Mayapur. My party of *brahmacharis* and I were called back to help organize. While in Calcutta we were invited to speak at Scottish Churches College, Prabhupada's alma mater. On the way there we noticed a woman begging in the street. She looked like a cross between Halle Berry and Sofia Loren in rags. Lying in front of her, asleep on the street, were four babies, obviously drugged.

One *brahmachari* went to offer her a *rupee,* but an Indian student said, "Don't do that."

"Why?"

"You've got to learn to say no."

When we arrived at Scottish Churches College I was with Dinanath Das, an American devotee and a fabulous *kirtan* singer. On the way to the college a pastor stopped him and put his hand on his shoulder.

"What's your name, son?"

"Dinanath."

"No, no. What's your Christian name?"

"Donald."

"Donald, are you happy? Really?"

Dinanath said, "I'm diving and surfacing in an ocean of transcendental nectar."

The pastor just stood speechless.

At the school auditorium two hundred upperclassmen cheered us on. The headmaster looked like Terry Thomas, same accent and gap between his teeth.

"There will be no chanting, of course," he said.

I gave a lecture about Prabhupada—"hometown boy does well" —and finished my talk saying, "So now chanting of Hare Krishna is going on all over the world except here. Your headmaster has forbidden it."

After a timid silence, the students broke into big applause. What student can't help getting it over on the principal?

"Thank you all, and everyone is invited to our international festival next week in Mayapur."

From the northern shore of Navadwip we could see scores of long boats full of people crossing the Ganges on their way to Mayapur. Our building in Mayapur housed over two thousand devotees from America, Europe, and Canada. Another thousand Indian devotees came. In our kitchen four cauldrons fabricated from half-inch-thick iron sheets fed thousands per day. Our chef could put more taste in his preparations for ten thousand people than most cooks could for ten. (We once asked him to cook a lunch for eight to ten people, but he refused.)

We printed five thousand invitation cards in full color. Prabhu-pada told me to take fifty of them to Tirtha Maharaj (a son of the mother) at his temple, the birthplace of Chaitanya Mahaprabhu. I went with two of my godbrothers. He was sitting with a few gentlemen when we arrived.

"We would like to invite the *sadhus* of the *math* to our temple." I handed him the invitations, and he said, "One copy will do."

"When I was in Calcutta," I said, "I met your cousin, who said one of your relatives had died and that . . ."

He cut me off. "I have no cousin; I am a *sannyasi*. I have no relatives."

We all smiled at his instructive answer, bowed, and left.

In the main hall on the first day, I spoke to the assembled devotees: "Here you can chant as loud as you want. The neighbors don't complain. Sages who live for a thousand years performing austerities attain liberation in Brahman. But here the devotees kick away that liberation as they dance and chant Hare Krishna and Gaura-hari."

At the birthsite of Chaitanya Mahaprabhu I explained our heritage.

At the *samadhi* (tomb) of our grandsire guru Gaurakishor Das Babaji two thousand devotees assembled. Although he was illiterate, pundits and yogis came to him for advice on the scriptures. He was extremely humble, and at the end of his life he said, "Tie a rope to my leg and drag my dead body through the streets of Navadwip like a dog so people can see what someone with no Krishna *bhakti* looks like."

The pseudo *babas* were going to do that. They planned to take his body, make his tomb a place of pilgrimage, and charge money to pilgrims. Then Bhaktisiddhanta arrived.

"I am his only disciple," he told them. "I am taking him to Mayapur. You are all so corrupt. But I will allow you to take him if any one of you can say you have not been with a woman in five years. Otherwise no one can touch him."

No answer.

"One year? One month? One day?"

No one responded.

"Then you cannot touch him."

"One by one they all skulked off," I told the large group of devotees. "Bhaktisiddhanta brought Gaurakishor Das Babaji's body here, where we are gathered."

At Bhaktivinode Thakur's home I read the prophecy he wrote almost a hundred years before: "Oh, for that day when the fortunate English, French, Russian, German, and American people will take up banners, *mridangas,* and *kartals* and raise *kirtan* through their streets and towns. When will that day come? Oh, for the day when the fair-skinned men from their side will raise up the chanting of *jaya sachinandan, jaya sachinandan ki jaya* [All glories to Lord Caitanya! All glories to Lord Caitanya!] and join with the Bengali devotees."

"So, to you Bhaktivinode Thakur, I say that day is today! Here we are!"

Then we began chanting names of Chaitanya: *jaya sachinandan gaurahari!* There was indescribable ecstasy as the gathering of over a thousand roared the names.

twelve
The Descending Process: Vaishnava Tantra

I

Vaishnavas accept two *tantras: Narada Pancharatra* and *Pancharatrika Vidhi.* These contain the rules and regulations to engage the material body, mind, and senses in the forms, names, qualities, and pastimes of Krishna. *Bhakti* yogis use their fingers to chant on beads, their tongue to taste *prasadam,* their sense of smell to smell flowers and incense offered to the Lord, their hands to care for tulasi trees, and their whole body to prostrate before the Deities, walk around sacred places, and perform ceremonies at various stages of life. There are sixty-four limbs of *bhakti* yoga described in Rupa Goswami's *Bhakti-rasamrita-sindhu,* which Prabhupada presented as *The Nectar of Devotion.* Vaishnava *tantras* control *vaidhi bhakti,* or devotion in practice. They bring one to the association of great devotees who can plant the seed of the spontaneous, natural, eternal function of the soul. Doing *Vaidhi bhakti* is like pushing and jump-starting a car with a weak battery. When the car reaches the right speed and its parts are in motion, then it starts up and the engine runs on its own power.

II

Durga, or Maha Maya, is the shadow of Krishna's divine energy, Yoga Maya, also known as Paurnamasi and Vrindadevi, after whom Krishna's abode is named: Vrindavan. Just as Durga manipulates the illusory material world of twenty-four dense and subtle elements, Yoga Maya manifests the abode of Krishna in the spiritual sky composed of only one element: spiritual energy. She is the executive director of the spiritual environment and all its paraphernalia.

Vishwanath sings, "O Vrinde! Radhika has given you dominion over Krishna's abode, which is the crown of the Vaikuntha planets."

The *Brahma Samhita* describes how Krishna consorts with hundreds and thousands of goddesses of fortune in the form of *gopis*. Radha-Krishna in Goloka Vrindavan are like a touchstone that generates gold, jewels, and precious minerals from anything that comes in contact with it. Just as the earth orbits around the sun, the sun orbits in the galaxy, and all the planets revolve around Polaris (the pole star, Dhruva Loka), similarly, all the Vaikuntha planets, in royal opulence, revolve around the supreme abode, Goloka Vrindavan. When Krishna is in His royal palace, He wears a crown and the garland of royal victory, Vaijayanti Mala. In Vrindavan He wears a peacock feather in His hair and a garland of forest flowers, Vana Mala.

Just as Krishna is the source of all incarnations, so Srimati Radha is the source of all ecstatic expansions of the queens of Dwarka and the queens of Vaikuntha, Lakshmi. Any pleasure experienced anywhere, even mundane pleasure, ultimately comes from Radha.

Someone once asked Srila Prabhupada a challenging question. "Can Krishna make a rock so heavy that He can't pick it up?" "Yes." "Then He is not all-powerful." Prabhupada answered, "Then He will pick it up." The challenger said, "Then He can't create a rock He can't lift." Prabhupada said, "Then He will create another rock, then lift it again, and again create and lift. Krishna is always expanding His energy, and then He measures it, then expands it again and measures it. This is the nature of Krishna's pastimes."

III

Who is more qualified than Durga to hear of the transcendental description of Radha, the ecstatic *hladini shakti, the origin of all energies?* Who is more qualified than Shiva to teach this knowledge? And what more vivid song is there than *Sri Radha Kripa Kataksha Stava Raja* from the *Urdhvamnaya Tantra* to convey this knowledge?

Sada Shiva and his consort Parvati, or Durga, have the following conversation below the Vaikuntha sky, just above the Causal Ocean—at the cusp, the point between matter and spirit. Vaishnavas in Vrindavan sing these tantric verses in the morning hours.

"O Srimati Radhika, consort of Sri Krishna! Topmost sages like Shukadeva, Narada, and Uddhava, are always offering prayers to Your lotus feet, remembering You, and praying for Your service, which miraculously removes all the miseries of sins and the offenses of the three modes of material nature. Your joyful face blooms like a lotus, and You delight in pastimes in the forests and groves of Braj. You are the daughter of Vrishabhanu Maharaj and are the dearly beloved of Brajendra Nandana Krishna, with whom You always play.

When will You bestow upon me Your merciful sidelong glance?

"In the immensely auspicious drama enacted with loving playfulness on the amorous battlefield, Your eyebrows, curving like bows, suddenly unleash the arrows of your sidelong glances, piercing Nanda Nandana Krishna with amorous delusion and bringing Him into eventual submission. In this way He eternally comes under Your complete control. O Radhika, when will You bestow that merciful sidelong glance upon me?

"Your soft arms are like fresh, delicate lotus stems elegantly swaying in the waves, just as a creeper dances in a gust of wind. Your restless bluish eyes flash in an enthralling glance. Your charm entices Krishna Himself to follow after You, and then in meeting, You steal away His mind and give Him shelter in His spellbound condition. When will You bestow Your sidelong glance upon me?

"As You walk along, Your captivating golden ankle bells sweetly resound with a host of Vedic mantras, resembling the warbling of a flock of royal swans. The beauty of Your limbs resembles undulating golden creepers. O Radharani, when will You bestow Your merciful sidelong glance upon me?

"You are worshiped as Sri Lakshmi, the goddess of unlimited millions of Vaikuntha planets. Sri Pavarti, Indrani, and Sarasvati all worship and attain benedictions from You. Meditation on even one of Your toenails grants an infinite variety of perfections. O Srimati Radhika, when will You bestow Your merciful sidelong glance upon me?"

IV

Bhaktivinode Thakur, our spiritual great-grandsire, said to a disciple, "The Vaishnavas who reside in holy places like Vrindavan and

Navadwip are wrong! I want to perform my deepest devotions at Kurukshetra."

"Why?" asked the disciple. "Do you want to remember the place where Krishna spoke the *Gita* to Arjuna?"

"No. In the age before the *Gita,* Kurukshetra was made sacred when the avatar Parasuram filled five lakes with the blood of the warrior caste. This was done to lighten the world overburdened by military might. But I am thinking of Krishna's time before the *Gita* and the battle between the Kauravas and Pandavas. Krishna resided in palaces of opulent splendor in Dwarka. While He reigned as Lord of the world, a great festival took place at Kurukshetra during a solar eclipse. All the royal families and powerful heroes assembled to celebrate there. They feasted on only pure foods, fried in *ghee*, like *kachoris.*"

Kurukshetra lies near Vrindavan. Hearing of the festival, Krishna's cowherd family and friends from Vrindavan took the opportunity to make the journey to Kurukshetra to see Krishna again after a very long time. Krishna met with many thousands of royal dignitaries, military generals, and heads of state, and He made some excuse to get away from the crowd to meet the Brajvasis. His brother, Balaram, and sister, Subhadra, had three chariots made ready to take Them to the secluded place where the Brajvasis had set up their camp, some distance away from the royal crowd.

Subhadra said, "I will go in the first chariot so they will see me and not think some big generals are arriving. Balaram, You go in the second chariot, and Krishna in the third. We will go slowly, so the chariots don't raise dust."

Arriving at the Brajvasi's camp, Krishna and Balaram met the residents of Vrindavan—Yashoda, Rohini, Maharaj Nanda, the cowherd boys—and satisfied them all with good wishes and happy memories of when He lived with them.

Then Krishna slipped away to an even more secluded grove to meet with His cowherd girlfriends, of whom the most beloved is Radha. Radha and Krishna are as inseparable as the sun and the sun's heat. The *Brihad Gautamiya Tantra* describes Sri Radha as nondifferent from Krishna. She presides over all goddesses of fortune. She is Krishna's internal ecstatic energy (*hladini shakti*). The essence of this potency gives ecstasy to Krishna and is called *prema* (divine love).

Krishna tries to pacify Radha, who is heartbroken by years of separation from Him. He tries to convince Her that He is always with Her because He is all-pervasive and is seated in Her heart as the Supersoul. He explains that He is within everything and everything is resting within Him. They can never be separate, as He would instruct Arjuna in the *Gita* in "those two verses" (in the ninth chapter). "Like fire stored in wood, I am in You always. There is no need for you to feel separation. "

Krishna is the supreme enjoyer, and Radha is the supreme enjoyable energy. She is *maha-bhava,* or the highest essence of *prema,* and can completely bewilder Krishna. At Kurukshetra, in the most intense state of *maha-bhava,* Radha rejects Krishna's instructions with affectionate anger: "That incompetent creator Brahma, who sprang from Your navel, created eyelids that obstruct our vision even for one moment's blinking. You have associated with that *Vedanta* pundit too long, and now Your intelligence seems to have been contaminated, so You have forgotten us. We are not yogis or sages or scholars of the *Vedas.* Your presence is in us as fire is in wood, but Your amorous glances are like lightning that burns and ignites our hearts. Take off Your royal crown, put a peacock feather in Your hair, abandon this military attitude, and return to Vrindavan. Play Your flute and dance again. We *gopis* are very envious of Your flute. What austerities did that yogi perform to take birth as an ordinary bamboo tree that gave birth to Your flute? Your lips are meant for us. Come back to Govardhan Hill. By the touch of Your lotus feet Govardhan trembled and all the trees and flowering bushes shook. Govardhan sheds tears of ecstasy, and the streams on his body carried flowers to us to make Your garlands."

Krishna now knows that His own energy has expanded beyond His own conception and He is unable to reciprocate.

"I, the Lord of the mind and yoga, gave the *gopis* the nectar of knowledge, but it could not extinguish the blazing fire of their love."

This statement has a dual purpose. It fools the nondevotee scholars, and it teaches the sincere devotees the confidentiality of *prema*.

Krishna wept.

"Day and night I think of You. I will return after performing a few more responsibilities."

The energy has surpassed the energetic—the rock He cannot lift. The transcendence has transcended itself. To respond to this, Krishna must taste the ecstasy of *maha-bhava,* His own pleasure potency (*hladini shakti*). Now Krishna must come as Chaitanya Mahaprabhu: Krishna combined with the golden complexion and *maha-bhava* (the most intense loving moods) of Radha.

V

Every year, Lord Chaitanya would celebrate the chariot festival in Jagannath Puri, Orissa. His golden form surrounded by thousands of devotees, He led them all in divine chanting and dancing as they joined Him in pulling the three enormous chariots of Subhadra, Balaram, and Jagannath (Krishna) from the Jagannath temple to the Gundicha temple. (See back cover photo.)

The Jagannath temple is as imposing as an emperor's fortress. Krishna reigns there in His aspect of regal, opulent splendor, the Lord of the universe. Every year the Deities are taken in chariots and brought in a grand procession from the Jagannath temple to the pastoral Gundicha temple, where the Deities are taken off the chariot and installed for a five-day festival. The Gundicha temple is situated in the midst of lush gardens with heavenly ponds full of fragrant flowers. Gundicha is Lord Jagannath's secluded pleasure garden, where He and His entourage celebrate informally in comfort for five days. His beloved consort Her Royal Highness Lakshmi Devi, the goddess of fortune, is never invited.

Chaitanya Mahaprabhu, whose eyes are always anointed with the unguent of transcendental love, envisioned the towering Jagannath temple as one of Krishna's palaces in Dwarka and saw the Gundicha temple and surrounding gardens as Vrindavan. Halfway in the procession from the Jagannath temple, He remembered the time in Kurukhsetra when Krishna, Balaram, and Subhadra came in three chariots to meet all the residents of Vrindavan.

His Royal Highness Sri Krishna, the Lord of the opulent city of Dwarka, the Lord of the universe, is always longing for His days in Braj Vrindavan when He played with the cowherd boys and His *gopis*. Once Rohini, the mother of Balaram, described the Braj pastimes to the queens in Dwarka. She told them to shut all the doors because these tales are very confidential and if Krishna hears them He may run away to Vrindavan. Krishna, Balaram, and Subhadra listened outside the door, side by side. Hearing about Braj, They melted in ecstasy. Their arms and legs sunk into Their torsos, and Their faces swelled into wide-eyed smiles. That is the form of the Jagannath Deity worshiped now in wood (*daru brahma*) and eternally fixed in ecstasy in the temple of Puri. When Mahaprabhu dances before the chariots, He is tasting His own ecstasy and distributing that to all. That is what makes Him dance! He is the same Krishna, dancing before Himself, and even Jagannath, the Deity, is astounded. Now Krishna, as Chaitanya, tastes the mood of Radha when She astounded Krishna at Kurukshetra.

> "You don't remember me, but I remember you.
> 'Twas not so long ago, you broke my heart in two . . .
> If we could start anew, I wouldn't hesitate.
> I'd gladly take you back and tempt the hand of fate . . ."
> —Little Anthony

At one point the chariots stopped. Even the royal elephants could not move them. To Lord Chaitanya's eyes this represented the moment when Krishna expressed to Radha His sorrow for having to delay His return to Vrindavan.

Then Mahaprabhu began to sing a verse from a mundane romance song that tells of a lover pleading to her beloved to return to the gardens where they first met. This astounded and bewildered all the devotees except for two confidential associates, Swarup Damodar and Rupa Goswami, who understood that Mahaprabhu was tasting the mood of Sri Radha. Rupa Goswami later rewrote the mundane song, knowing it to have the same sentiment as the prayer of Radha to Krishna when They'd met at Kurukshetra five thousand years before. Mahaprabhu pushed the chariot with His head, and it seemed to move by itself on its path to the groves of the Gundicha temple. He led the devotees in ecstatic dancing and singing. Arriving at Gundicha, He and His associates stayed for the five-day festival in ecstatic celebration with Krishna in the gardens of the Gundicha temple (Vrindavan).

VI

One morning in the spring of 1975 I accompanied Prabhupada on a morning walk with a large group of devotees in the spacious park of the Victoria Memorial, Calcutta.

As we walked past the gleaming white marble imperial palace, Prabhupada said, "During British times this open field was not made for strolling only, but also to make a clear path for the battery cannon fire. Many Indian revolutionaries were publicly executed on this field, Oh, yes. All the big British *sahibs* would meet with the Maharajas here. When I was young I saw King George V come through this park. Thousands of people attended, and all were given cups with fresh *kachoris* fried in *ghee*. I remember mine had one *kachori* and two sweets in it. I was a schoolboy then, and the teachers brought us all to greet the king of Great Britain. We students shouted, *jaya raj, raj ki jaya.*"

There were Maharajas on elephants and in their cars. But for King George the British arranged a red carpet two miles long, not for him to walk on, but for his car—a big Rolls Royce—to ride. The British exploited India like anything. The expression was, "If you want to see the wealth of India, look at the British crown jewels."

Prabhupada then spoke about New York in 1966.

"That is where we started. You remember how Mukunda got me that store and the apartment. There was that nice small garden where we took *prasadam* sometimes. We all used one towel. You were cooking. When I had the heart attack, you helped me. Raymond was doing the printing. Brahmananda was working. He one time carried hundred pounds rice bag up the stairs. Jadurani was painting, Gargamuni was eating. There was some struggle, but it was sweet."

In 1977, in the eighty-second year of his manifested pastimes, His Divine Grace A. C. Bhaktivendanta Swami Prabhupada reentered his eternal pastimes. He whose heart I had massaged, who had taught me how to cook, read scripture, chant, and worship Krishna, and who answered my questions, is no longer visible to my mundane vision.

In the sixteenth century, Raghunath Das Goswami lived on after other intimate disciples of Lord Chaitanya had passed away. Raghunath wrote of his grief on the passing of Srila Rupa Goswami: "I thought, 'If I go to all the ecstatic places of Radha-Krishna's pastimes, perhaps that will ease my grief.' But when I got up after bowing to Radha Kunda, I saw instead of a beautiful lake only the dark open mouth of a tiger. In fear, I turned to Shyama Kund, only to see the open jaws of a lion ready to eat me. I then went running to Govardhan Hill, and there, instead of a holy mountain, I saw the open jaws of a python ready to swallow me up. Nothing can console me now that I know that I will never see my Guru Maharaj again in this life."

Epilogue

I n my book of Vaishnava *acharyas'* songs, Narottama sings, "Where will I ever find personalities as magnanimous as Lord Chaitanya and His associates?" Devotees always feel the sentiment that there will never again be such personalities, and yet they appear century after century, age after age.

It is the Vaisnava's tradition to be innovative, not fixed in religious ritual. Krishna came as a fish; a tortoise; a half man, half lion; and Himself, to carry out what was necessary. As the Vrindavan devotees say, Prabhupada's spiritual perfection was already fulfilled when he took *sannyas,* translated the *Bhagavatam* into English, and lived at the Radha-Damodar temple, the holiest place in Vrindavan. Yet in his seventieth year he felt he had not done enough to fulfill his spiritual master's orders, so he sailed to America at great risk.

At the time of this writing, it has been thirty-four years since his departure from this world, and many of my godbrothers and godsisters have spread Krishna consciousness all over the world. I believe even demigods from the upper planetary systems are cutting their long lives short to be born as Vaishnavas on this Bhumi-loka (earth planet), and great Vaishnavas who have not quite yet completed their devotion and wish to taste the nectar of spreading the holy name and enter into the fire of this preaching movement, are being born—some revealing themselves, others not—and many still to come.

Appendix: These Are a Few Of My Favorite Things

Prabhupada's Zingers

(I think this first one is the best.) Prabhupada said, "Study my books very carefully because after I'm gone people will say, 'Prabhupada said this, Prabhupada said that.'"

"Anyone who doesn't believe in God is either a madman or a fool number one. You want proof? Every day is proof."

Mundane logic cannot help you realize the Absolute Truth: "At night, can you find the sun? Even with a hundred-power flashlight you cannot see the sun, and when the sun is in the sky, what is the use of your flashlight?"

"When we feel a breeze, is that Krishna's breath?" a devotee asked. "Yes, that is Krishna consciousness."

A devotee said, "I only have faith in you, Prabhupada." Prabhupada said, "Just have faith in Krishna; even I may disappoint you."

"It is the business of Maya to make this Krishna consciousness movement look ridiculous."

"We don't give up anything; we add Krishna."

Prabhupada was often asked, "Do I have to give up my job and become an ascetic?"
Prabhupada said, "We do not practice severe austerities. Every season a snake sheds its old skin because the new skin has been made. If you cut the new skin, the snake will die. Chanting Hare Krishna will give a higher taste. The old desires will fall away."

"What you learn easily is easy to forget. What you learn with difficulty will be difficult to forget."

One of Prabhupada's godbrothers who did not travel to the West said, "If Lord Chaitanya wanted to preach Krishna around the world, why didn't He go Himself?"
Prabhupada boldly said, "Because He saved that glory for me!"

"I have written more knowledge than is possible to absorb in a lifetime."

In Europe Prabhupada became very ill, and in his sickness he turned to a devotee and said, "A man—struggling with Krishna's plan."

Prabhupada told how riches cannot save one from death: "You may be Rockefeller; you may be any feller. Death is certain."

A professor was arguing about the inaccuracy of the oral tradition. Prabhupada said, "Written language is a symptom of forgetfulness."

"If it cannot be said in simple words, it is bogus."

"There are so many flags in front of the United Nations. Where is the united? When there is one flag, it will be united."

After the movement got very successful worldwide there was a lot of money, and he said, "Now, getting money is not difficult. Spending it properly is difficult."

"To have brotherhood of man there must be fatherhood of God."

"You all want to see God; why not hear God?"

After we'd written and printed four or five issues of *Back to Godhead* magazine, we asked the Swami, "Would you write an article for *Back to Godhead* magazine?"
His answer demonstrated the principle of simultaneous oneness and difference, a central doctrine of Chaitanya's philosophy.
"Are all your articles based on what you have heard from me?"
"Yes."
"Then I write all the articles."

"Hare Krishna *maha-mantra* is not a something; it is a somebody."

On Krishna's personal and impersonal features: "The lawyer says to the judge, 'May it please the court.' The judge is a man and the entire court simultaneously. The judge is also called 'the bench.' Is a judge a bench? No. When the lawyer puts something 'to the bench,' does it just stay on the judge's desk? No, it means it will be read by the judge."

A disciple said, "I'm going to renounce the world."
"You do not own the world, so how can you renounce it?
Everything belongs to Krishna, not us. Knowing that is renunciation."

A disciple asked, "How do the three modes control the living
entities"
"Do you know why dogs run?"
"Why?"
"No reason."

A devote asked, "Can we just read your books?"
Prabhupada tugged the devotee's ear. "Book cannot do this!"

"Prabhupada, what is the difference between the mind and the
intelligence?"
"When you look down from a tall building and your mind says
jump, your intelligence says don't."

"You want to see God? Do something so that God will want to see
you."

Srila Prabhupada and I were having *darshan* of the newly installed
Deities in Calcutta. Glancing at Prabhupada, I saw his face beam-
ing with a huge smile. I noticed that Krishna's flute was backwards.
I said, "They placed the flute the wrong way."
Still smiling, he said, "Krishna is all-powerful; He can play from
either end."

"Krishna is in the world but untouched by it. Just like a spider—
the insects are trapped, but the spider can walk freely over the web;
he is not trapped.

On a morning walk in Honolulu: "It is not possible to be completely happy in this material world, but maybe in Hawaii."

We asked Prabhupada about bogus gurus, and he said, "Of course, if they are bogus they cannot be guru, but you should not reject a bona fide guru. You may see a counterfeit coin; it does not mean we stop using money."

After a lucid lecture of logical conclusions, Prabhupada asked, "Are there any questions?
After a brief silence, with a beaming smile he said, "How can there be any questions?"

"Nothing is separate from God; that's all right. We are one in quality with God, but we do not become God."
He licked his hand and said, "It is like saying I am salty, so I am the ocean."

In 1966 a gentleman approached Prabhupada to sell him a historic building once owned by Alexander Hamilton. It turned out to be a false proposition. Prabhupada said, "I never liked him. He kept calling me 'Your Excellency.' The flatterer is your enemy."

"Serving Krishna is like watering the root of a tree. All the branches and leaves are nourished. Similarly, if you have a million dollars, all your ten-dollar problems are solved."

"But how can an all-loving God allow suffering?" someone asked. Prabhupada replied, "When the sun sets, the thieves come out. Is the sun to blame? Everything is created by God. If you use His energy for yourself, you are a thief."

Prabhupada told a manager of several temples, "You are moving around too much. None of your centers are doing well. You must stay in one temple until it is fully developed; if not, then die there. A rolling stone gathers no moss. Now you must gather some moss."

A disciple asked, "Is there one special day of the week that is holy like Sunday?"
Prabhupada replied, "Every day with Krishna is a holy day."

A challenging question: "If you say you have full knowledge, then how many windows are in the Empire State Building?"
Prabhupada challenged back, "How many drops of water are in a mirage?"

"But, Srila Prabhupada, I have so many doubts."
"Doubt is a symptom of intelligence. This is not blind-faith dogma; ask any question."

Someone told Prabhupada that many people in America were on diets and weight-loss pills.
"Don't eat so much!" was his solution.

"To say that God is void and to say there is no God is the same thing."

An eccentric man boasted, "I am fearless. I am God!"
"Do you cross the street at the green light?'
"Sure."
"Then you are afraid of death."

"Western science is only involved with energy. We are involved with the energetic, Krishna. When you have knowledge of the energetic, then the energy is properly understood."

"Too much dependence on others shortens one's duration of life."

"Proprietorship turns sand into gold."

"So why are there so many different religions? Which one is real?" "You have the pocket dictionary and the ten-thousand-page dictionary. The pocket edition is not wrong, but the library edition is more complete."

"You may have a thousand thousand zeros, but they all add up to zero. Put a one in front, and there is value."
(In other words, material assets have real value only when used in Krishna's service.)

"You have to be very strict; you have to be very liberal."

"In the service of Krishna, you can put your feet on my head."

My Zinger: *"Prema bhakti, raga bhakti, bhava bhakti* must have the comprehensive knowledge of the science of Krishna's unlimited potencies, qualities, and pastimes of all His incarnations. It is not just idly talking only about His love *lila* with the *gopis*. It is the love that inspires a penniless seventy-year-old holy man to take a thirty-five-day freighter voyage to an unknown country and start a worldwide mission from nothing."

ACKNOWLEDGEMENTS

I would like to thank the following people for their encouragement and assistance with this project:

Jay Hari Dasi (Jeanette Hinsdale)—transcribing
Nagaraj Das—editing
Yamaraj Das—layout and design
Pundarik Vidyanidhi Das, Kaliyapani Das,
    and Mukhara Dasi—proofreading
Lilananda Das (Joe Santos)—for providing the computer
Brahmatirtha Das (Bob Cohen), Yogesvara Das
    (Joshua M. Greene), Balavanta Das (William Ogle),
    and Krishna Gopal Das—for their generous donations
Hansarupa Das (Jeff Moy)—for providing all life's necessities